STORIES ARE WEAPONS

ALSO BY ANNALEE NEWITZ

Nonfiction

Four Lost Cities:
A Secret History of the Urban Age

Scatter, Adapt, and Remember:
How Humans Will Survive a Mass Extinction

Novels

The Terraformers

The Future of Another Timeline

Autonomous

STORIES ARE WEAPONS

PSYCHOLOGICAL WARFARE AND THE AMERICAN MIND

ANNALEE
NEWITZ

W. W. NORTON & COMPANY

Independent Publishers Since 1923

For information about permission to reproduce selections from this book, write to
Permissions, W. W. Norton & Company, Inc., 500 Fifth Avenue, New York, NY 10110

For information about special discounts for bulk purchases, please contact
W. W. Norton Special Sales at specialsales@wwnorton.com or 800-233-4830

Manufacturing by Lakeside Book Company
Book design by Daniel Lagin
Production manager: Delaney Adams

ISBN 978-0-393-88151-6

W. W. Norton & Company, Inc., 500 Fifth Avenue, New York, N.Y. 10110
www.wwnorton.com

W. W. Norton & Company Ltd., 15 Carlisle Street, London W1D 3BS

1 2 3 4 5 6 7 8 9 0

For anyone who has been told that they should not be alive.
Together we will survive this war.

CONTENTS

PREFACE:
THE BRAIN FOG OF WAR

t's hard to write about a war while it's raging. Especially when there are no craters in the ground, no missiles streaking overhead— just words and images that are inflicting a form of psychological damage that is impossible to measure, impossible to prove. When I started researching this book in mid-2020, the world was locked down in a pandemic that was unleashing a torrent of propaganda the likes of which I had never seen. As a friend of mine lay dying of COVID on a ventilator, President Donald Trump promised that we could cure the disease with light and deworming medication for horses. After police killed George Floyd, I watched as disinformation about the Black Lives Matter movement piled up on social media,[1] where anonymous accounts falsely blamed protesters for violence.[2] A conspiracy theory from 2016 about pizza-eating pedophiles radicalized a huge number of right-wing extremists, who later joined crowds storming the Capitol, trying to murder the vice president and overturn the 2020 presidential election. And then the media itself began to implode. Tech billionaire Elon Musk bought Twitter—once a key part of America's digital public sphere—and turned it into a bizarro right-wing propaganda machine in a matter of months. OpenAI, the company that created the ChatGPT app, warned that its product might cause the apocalypse—then funded a studio that would help newspapers use it to replace journalists.[3]

Every time I thought I had a handle on what was happening, some new development would send me into a spiral of nihilism. The Supreme Court overturned *Roe v. Wade*, destroying the universal access to legal abortion that so many of us had taken for granted our whole lives. Anti-trans ideology insinuated its way into public policy, and I started to make lists of states where my friends and I couldn't go to the bathroom, couldn't get health care, couldn't speak publicly without risking arrest for being in "drag." It wasn't just scary—it was absurd. Around this time, an avowedly racist Air Force National Guardsman leaked classified US intelligence about the Ukraine War on a Discord server devoted to the game Minecraft. I felt like I was in a war zone, or maybe a satirical movie about a war zone, waiting for the next bomb to drop.

Through it all, I was trying to write my way out of the terror and confusion. I knew that I had to stop living in the moment, stop feeling the dread, and put what was happening to the United States in a deeper context. I turned to history for answers, researching American ideological conflicts of the past two hundred years—from formal military psychological operations to messy domestic culture wars—hoping to find precedents that would explain why our democracy was devolving into what felt like madness. As a science journalist, I was frustrated that there were no scientific instruments, no objective measures I could use to prove that people's lives were being destroyed by words and ideas. But as a fiction writer, I knew there were other ways to get at the truth, to make sense of a world gripped by absurdity and chaos. I had to tell a story.

ALIENS AND PSYCHIC WARS

A red-tipped tower dominates the skyline of Stanford University. Surrounded by low-slung Spanish colonial architecture and tree-shaded sidewalks, this missile-shaped building is part of the Hoover Institution on War, Revolution, and Peace, a conservative think tank founded in 1919 by Herbert Hoover. I first visited the place on a windy fall day in 2021, in that brief period between the Delta and Omicron waves of COVID when things were opening up in the Bay Area. My destination was a sunken courtyard at the root of the tower, which led to a basement-level floor entirely occupied by the Hoover Institution Archives. Scholars, heads of state, and policy wonks from all over the world come to the archive to study its extensive collection of documents related to propaganda and psychological warfare.

To enter the archive, I passed through two security checkpoints—one to verify my identity and check my vaccination status, and the other to show the librarians that I carried only a computer, a phone, and a pencil. No backpacks, no sweaters with pockets, and absolutely no permanent markers are permitted at the Hoover Institution Library & Archives. If I wanted to write something down, the librarian told me, I could use the official yellow Hoover Institution paper. Before I exited the security gauntlet, a staffer took my picture and made a special "reader card" ID for me. If I left to use the bathroom or grab some lunch, I'd need to flash my card to get back in. The vibe was a cross between an intelligence agency and a museum.

I had come to sift through the personal papers of an odd military intelligence expert named Paul Linebarger, who wrote a handbook called *Psychological Warfare* for the US Army in the late 1940s that came to define modern psychological operations in the United States. Though few people know his name, his book is still recommended reading today at Fort Liberty,[4] where Special Operations soldiers are trained to influence and deceive their enemies. When I brought the first archival box of his papers to my assigned desk, slipping on gloves to protect the century-old diaries and photos inside, I was plunged into a Cold War mystery. Like many intelligence experts, Linebarger led a few secret lives, but his covert identities were not for the spycraft you might expect. Instead, they were entirely for the purpose of telling stories. Under the pseudonym Felix C. Forrest, he wrote literary fiction about women's lives that one reviewer described as "like pages from a psychiatrist's notebook";[5] as Carmichael Smith, he penned a Cold War spy novel called *Atomsk*; and as Cordwainer Smith, he wrote dozens of science fiction stories and novels that made him a cult figure in the 1950s and '60s.

I read through years of his personal diaries, his classified research, and his critically acclaimed stories about a ruthless future space empire called the Instrumentality. There were his grade-school notebooks devoted to studying Chinese, which he learned while his diplomat father was stationed in China, right alongside classified documents related to the adult Linebarger's deployment during World War II. He studied psychology and political subterfuge with equal relish. In one folder, I found an unpublished book called "Ethical Dianetics," written under the name Carmichael Smith, in which he proposed a radical system of "mutual emotional aid." In another was a detailed report on how the United States should secretly foment "passive resistance" to communism in China during the Cold War. During World War II, he kept a journal of keen observations from his travels. Some were about how the war affected the many countries he visited, from Asia to Africa, but some were simply arresting images. In 1943, passing through Sudan, he wrote, "At [Al Fashir], U.S. officers flocked to see women working on building construction." He was acutely aware of the kinds of cultural differences that arouse curiosity—and outrage. Still, most of his published output was fiction, rather than treatises like *Psychological Warfare*.

Why did he write about fantastical wars in outer space when he had so much to say about wars on Earth? The more I immersed myself in Linebarger's work, the more obvious it became that his skill as a science fiction writer was a crucial part of his success with military psyops. Propaganda is, after all, a story we tell to win allies and frighten enemies. The more compelling and emotionally engaging the story is, the more people will want to read, watch, or listen to it. Linebarger believed that words, properly deployed, were more powerful than bombs. In the Army, and at the Johns Hopkins University School of Advanced International Studies, he taught two generations of soldiers how to weaponize stories to benefit the United States and its interests. His goal wasn't to browbeat people into obedience with slogans and threats. He used a surprising amount of nuance and rationality mixed with entertainment to persuade his audiences to ally with the United States. Linebarger connected with audiences however he could, whether by secreting his ideas inside science fiction stories or by laying them out in classified reports.

Sitting in the quiet Hoover Institution Library & Archives, I glanced up occasionally at my fellow researchers in their professorial tweeds or the scruffy jeans of impoverished grad students. Outside, in the courtyard, a cool breeze ruffled the manicured trees. I felt briefly that meditative sense one sometimes gets in academic institutions, as if we were insulated from the world and completely safe.

But we weren't safe.

All of us in that room and beyond were feeling pain, or at the very least unease, as America's ongoing psychological battles erupted around the economy, health care, schools, the courts, and in government at all levels. We were all in a heightened state of fight-or-flight. The more I learned, the more convinced I was that storytelling was to blame. On a 2022 episode of the book-centric podcast *Print Run*, literary agents Laura Zats and Erik Hane pointed out that it's common to describe a story as "feel-good," but people rarely admit there are also "feel-bad" stories that wound us emotionally.[6] Obviously if a story can make you feel better or smarter, it can also make you feel worse and more confused. And if that story can change your behavior—whether in the voting booth or on the street—it becomes a weapon.

Today in the United States, psywar is virtually indistinguishable from culture war. One might liken the situation to what happened when federal programs in the 1990s made it cheap and easy for police departments to acquire unused military equipment like semiautomatic weapons and tanks.[7] Weapons intended for use in combat zones are now being deployed in the American suburbs.

Peter Pomerantsev, author of *This Is Not Propaganda*, points out that military influence operations have bled over into civilian conflicts, creating a "flood of disinformation and deception, 'fake news,' [and] 'information war.'"[8] When we use psyops in our cultural conflicts, we tear down the wall between what's appropriate in domestic disagreements among Americans and what's acceptable in combat against a foreign enemy.

As a science journalist and fiction author, I've spent most of my life at the crossroads between hard realities and the fantasies we entertain about them. Psychological warfare and culture war exist at this crossroads too. Linebarger argued in his work that successful propaganda always contains a slice of the truth: it refers to actual events and true histories, but decontextualizes them, relocates them to an imaginary terrain of mythical good guys and bad guys. And that's why it gets us in our hearts and guts.

PSYOP VS. PSYOP

Psychological warfare has no known origin story. By the time the Chinese classic *The Art of War* was written, likely 2,500 years ago,[9] the practice was already widely used and complex. Often ascribed to a philosopher and military general named Sun Tzu or Master Sun, *The Art of War* describes tactics like deception and distraction, which today might be called disinformation, propaganda, or special operations. More than anything else, *The Art of War* is about psychological strategies—some diplomatic, some sneaky—that a good leader should use to avoid violence. Linebarger, who spent part of his childhood in China and was a scholar of Chinese history, adopted this as his own credo while codifying the art of modern psychological warfare. He advised his students and fellow military officers to use psywar in order to prevent bloodshed.

Still, it's important to keep in mind that one goal of psychological warfare *is* to hurt the enemy—otherwise you're not striking a blow, you're just exchanging words. Psyops create the emotional agony and social ruptures of a kinetic war, without anyone firing a single shot. There are many ways to do this, and operatives have refined their tactics over time.

The nascent United States was the beneficiary of a new insight about psychological war, which was that confusion could act as a form of disinformation. It was an idea that stemmed from a growing awareness that European wars were far more chaotic and unpredictable than they had ever been. Carl von Clausewitz, in the first volume of his influential 1832 series *On War*, described battles where commanders were trapped in "a fog of greater or lesser uncertainty." What he meant was that commanders often had to make life-and-death decisions in an instant, without enough intelligence about the larger conflict or even the state of their own armies.[10] Later commentators like Colonel Lonsdale Hale,[11] referencing Clausewitz, began to describe this problem simply as "the fog of war."[12] The military quickly realized that uncertainty and chaos could also be weaponized. When an enemy is confused by multiple conflicting accounts of what's happening, they are vulnerable and easily manipulated. They no longer trust their sources of news, but are desperate for information. A skilled propagandist can step into the breach and provide it, misleading their targets into turning against their fellow citizens or surrendering to their would-be conquerors.

Though the United States used irregular, or unconventional,

warfare strategies throughout the Revolutionary War and the nineteenth-century Indian Wars, there was no formal term for these kinds of operations. It wasn't until World War I that the US War Department established the Psychologic Subsection of its Intelligence Division. In 1918, under the leadership of Captain Heber Blankenhorn and his deputy, the journalist Walter Lippmann, the division was renamed the Propaganda Section.[13] The Propaganda Section was responsible for creating millions of leaflets, dropped from airplanes like text bombs, intended to undermine the morale of German troops. The Intelligence Division was also tasked with censoring of the news, which is essentially another misinformation tactic. At that time, the terms "propaganda" and "psychological operations" were used interchangeably, but that would soon change.

After World War I, psychological operations, or psyops, became more closely associated with the military, while propaganda came to mean something far more slippery. Edward Bernays, an adman who conducted secret work for the US government, wrote a book called *Propaganda* in 1928 where he argued that propaganda has an "unpleasant connotation" but is merely "the mechanism by which ideas are disseminated on a large scale ... [in] an organized effort to spread a particular belief or doctrine." For Bernays and his many adherents, propaganda was part of everyday communication, no more remarkable than an iPhone ad or the *New York Times* op-ed section. Nearly any idea that was transmitted through mass media could be considered propaganda. Lippmann, who had witnessed military propaganda firsthand during the war, disagreed. He believed that propaganda was more coercive than journalism or advertising. Their disagreement persists among experts to this day, which is why so much political propaganda goes unchecked—it exists in a gray area between psyops and advertising.

It wasn't until World War II that psychological war activities gained a permanent home in the military, thanks to the establishment of the Army's Office of War Information, where Linebarger worked. At that point, many informal practices became military doctrine. The military loves an acronym, so the colloquial term "psyops" quickly became PSYOP in military documents, and psychological warfare became PSYWAR. Today, the Army has rebranded PSYOP as MISO, or military information support operations. An Army teaching manual for MISO soldiers from 2014 describes MISO as targeting foreign audiences "to elicit behaviors favorable to U.S. national objectives."[14] The Army's 8th Psychological Operations Group describes their mandate in more visceral terms on their website: "Masters of influence. Experts in deception."[15] Here I'll be using "PSYOP" only in the context of military doctrine where the term was used; I'll use lowercase "psyops" and "psywar" to refer to a broad range of irregular combat actions aimed at destabilizing a foreign power.

ALL-AMERICAN PSYWAR

We'll begin our exploration of psychological war by going back to its origins in the United States. In this country, psyops have always been connected to the evolving media industry. We'll meet Cold War propagandists who were moonlighting as fiction writers, and a Jazz Age adman who led psyops campaigns. Going back further, we'll see how the nineteenth-century Indian Wars created a uniquely American paradigm for psychological operations, which combined military action with media misrepresentations. The United States fought hundreds of Indigenous nations with guns as well as disinformation about Indigenous life in fiction, newspapers, and local histories. What the military didn't expect was that Indigenous nations in the West would clap back with their own psychological campaigns, such as the Ghost Dance movement, inspiring a new kind of activism that continues to this day.

Military psyops exist on a continuum with advertising and popular media. Together, this troika of influence machines tempts and coerces us into changing our behavior on a mass scale. While I researched this book, I took a class from a PSYOP instructor in the Army, who taught me to generate psychological "products" for "target audiences," a process modeled on advertising campaigns. His lessons helped explain why online advertising fueled one of the most explosive psychological wars of the twenty-first century. In the lead-up to the 2016 presidential race, Russian operatives used Facebook to reach over 126 million Americans with highly targeted ads, content, and memes. Their intent was to create chaos—much like the fog of war—but also to discourage Black people from voting.[16] This campaign didn't end with Trump's election. It's ongoing. We'll see how digital psywar has incorporated new tactics and is changing the way people use social media.

Next we'll track how the military's psychological weapons found their way into the rhetoric and tactics of culture warriors. Culture wars aren't waged by a state authority the way psychological wars are, though they often serve the interests of a government or another powerful institution like a church or corporation. Sometimes combatants are part of political movements. But mostly the people participating in these campaigns view themselves as fighting for truth or simply "telling it like it is." They don't always realize that they're contributing to a systemic cultural assault. Cultural operations can be deployed by many sources, from entertainment media and schools to scientific journals and public policy. But they all share the same goal: whipping up emotions against an enemy.

There are three major psychological weapons that combatants often transfer into culture war: scapegoating, deception, and violent threats. These weapons are what separate an open, democratic public debate from a psychological attack. In a militarized culture war, combatants will scapegoat specific groups of Americans by painting them as foreign adversaries; next, these culture warriors will lace their rhetoric with lies and bully their adversaries with threats of violence or imprisonment. We'll look at how this weapons transfer took place in some of the past century's devastating culture wars over American identity, zeroing in on conflicts over race and intelligence, school board fights over LGBT students, and activist campaigns to suppress feminist stories. In every case, we see culture warriors singling out specific groups of Americans, like Black people or trans teens, and bombarding them with psyops products as if they were enemies of the state.

Increasingly, Americans are not engaging in democratic debate with one another; they are launching weaponized stories directly into each other's brains. But we have the power to decommission those weapons. The final section of this book deals with the pathway to peace. How exactly do we issue a cease-fire in wars of the mind? The first edition of Linebarger's book *Psychological Warfare* ends with a manifesto on the importance of psychological disarmament. He believed that the purpose of psyops was to end war, not to ignite an infinite series of culture wars that would grind the nation to a halt. His ideas echoed key political philosophers of the Cold War era, like Jürgen Habermas and Herbert Marcuse, who argued that nations around the world needed to rebuild a shattered public sphere. Linebarger believed that the public sphere— the shared cultural realm where Americans swap ideas, tell stories, and build consensus through democratic elections—had been rotted by years of disinformation and violent manipulation. To start the reconstruction process, Linebarger suggested investing in public education, opening national borders, and supporting a robust free press. It's hard to imagine a career military man, intensely loyal to the US government his entire life, writing those words now. More specifically, it's hard to imagine him being heard. America's twenty-first-century culture warriors, led by politicians and media influencers, aim to flood the public sphere with chaos and slam our borders shut.

And yet even now, there is a counternarrative that promises something else. If we pay attention we can find it everywhere, suggesting practical, healthy ways to move beyond constant warfare to find a moment of peace. The term "healthy" is important here, because recovery from psywar requires what can only be called collective therapy. Psychological and culture wars cause trauma— that is their intent. Harvard psychologist Judith Herman, author of *Trauma and Recovery*, argues that we must first remember what has happened before we can move on.[17] That's why historical receipts, true accounts of our nation's past, are part of psychological disarmament. We'll meet an anthropologist, Coquille tribal chief Jason Younker, whose youthful adventures with a Xerox machine in the dusty basement of the National Archives in Washington, DC, restored his tribe's lost claims to land in southwest Oregon. He and his team uncovered documents that began a reconciliation process whose effects are being felt throughout the Pacific Northwest.

To achieve psychological disarmament, we'll need to rethink the role of stories in our lives—and, more importantly, to change the way we act on the stories we hear. This is especially true when it comes to the way we interact with online media, which is full of viral misinformation. How do we separate the goofball fakery from trustworthy sources? We'll hear from experts like Alex Stamos, former head of the Stanford Internet Observatory, who helped produce a national report on how to quell the tide of online disinformation about voting. He and his colleagues suggest using moderation systems that treat influence operations like email spam—filtering out the propaganda junk so that we can find the legitimate information we need. Other researchers, like Safiya Umoja Noble, author of *Algorithms of Oppression*, urge consumers to consider a "slow media" approach where we choose our media mindfully, analyzing it and testing its veracity before we swallow it whole.

There's a pervasive anxiety in the United States—and, sometimes, a hope—that people will imitate what they find in the stories they consume. It's why policymakers argue that kids playing violent games could become school shooters. It's also why right-wing pundits worry that teens reading about trans characters in young adult books might become trans themselves. In the United States, we treat fiction as politics—and vice versa. As a result, it's difficult for us to build a public sphere where we can come to a consensus about what's true rather than which story we like best. This conundrum leads us back to where we began: storytelling. As journalist Nesrine Malik argues in *We Need New Stories*,[18] culture wars have flooded our public sphere with tales built on "consensual dishonesty," or lies based on a shared mythical past. One way out of this prison house of mythology is to seek narratives that describe plausible democratic futures based on justice and repair. We'll explore "applied science fiction," a form of storytelling that pushes back against dystopian visions by describing ways to fix the world, rather than gawking at its smoking ruins. Ideas from these stories can spill over into public policy, which I would argue is a form of applied science fiction. Policies are visions of possible futures, attempts to change reality by imagining a different world.

The stories we tell one another using words, images, and theatrics are dual use. In peacetime, they can be sheer entertainment. During periods of conflict, they can destroy lives and topple nations. But war cannot, must not, last forever. This book is a story about how one nation, the United States, turned people's minds into blood-soaked battlegrounds—and how we, the people, can put down our weapons and build something better.

PART I

PSYOPS

CHAPTER 1

THE MIND BOMB

Modern psychological warfare began in the plush Vienna offices of an early twentieth-century doctor named Sigmund Freud, who popularized a new scientific discipline called psychoanalysis. In his writing and lectures, Freud argued that psychoanalysis had identified "the unconscious," a veiled part of the mind that motivates people even when they aren't aware of it. For Freud, unconscious desires were the key to understanding why people developed mental health problems, or "neuroses," as he liked to call them. With the help of a doctor like himself, trained in psychoanalysis, that desire could be made conscious and therefore controllable. He had some success with patients suffering from what therapists today would likely call depression and trauma. But many enthusiastic Freudians used his work in contexts that the doctor never intended, like advertising and wartime propaganda. No doubt he would have psychoanalyzed the hell out of these misappropriations, but he never got the chance. Freud died in 1939, shortly after Nazis drove him and his family out of Vienna.

Freud wanted to cure neuroses by helping people understand themselves—especially the taboo desires hidden in their unconscious minds. His form of therapy involved asking patients about their dreams, early memories, and fantasies; it was his way of plumbing their unconscious minds, where desire can roam free. He called it the "talking cure." Patients would narrate their own lives and analyze the arcane symbolism of their dreams, slowly piecing together all the events and feelings that had caused their troubles. Once the patient had a coherent story about themselves, Freud believed, they could work through whatever harmful thoughts or behaviors plagued them. If, however, they did not reengineer what Freud called the "mechanism" of their consciousness,[1] they were liable to be aggressive, depressed, self-destructive, or delusional. It turned out this also made them easy targets for propaganda.

We know that because savvy advertising creatives in New York City conducted what amounted to mass psychological experiments in the 1920s, when they started using Freud's ideas to sell products. The most prominent among them was Freud's own nephew, Edward Bernays, often heralded as the creator of "public relations" as a field. Bernays grew up in New York City, though he spent summers with Freud's family in the Alps—the two families were close, perhaps because all the parents were related. Bernays's mother was Freud's sister, and Bernays's father was the brother of Freud's wife. In 1917, Bernays sent his uncle a box of the Havana cigars he loved, and the psychoanalyst returned the favor by sending his nephew a copy of his latest book, *Introductory Lectures on Psycho-Analysis.* Though Freud's previous books had made waves in the scientific community, this was his first mainstream hit. The short book popularized Freud's conception of the unconscious and its connection to dreams. It also paved the way for Bernays's own meditation on psychology in 1923 called *Crystallizing Public Opinion*, which was about how to persuade the public by using mass media like newspapers to appeal to their unconscious biases.

One of Bernays's early career triumphs was an advertising campaign for Lucky Strike cigarettes in 1929, aimed specifically at young women. Smoking had long been considered a male habit, and it was generally taboo for women to smoke publicly. Bernays wanted to change all that and open up a new market for cigarettes. Freud had taught Bernays that the dream logic of the unconscious mind included a kind of emotional free association, where desire for one thing could easily morph into desire for something completely different—at least, if the two desires could be made to intertwine somehow. His only question was, what did women want, and how could Bernays convert it into a hankering for cigarettes? Young women in America at that time were still electrified by the success of the suffrage movement and were excited to pursue the newfound freedoms that came with the voting rights they had secured in 1920. So Bernays decided to create a campaign that could sublimate women's love of freedom into a lust for cigarettes. All he needed was the perfect mass media vehicle—one that fed women's dreams. He worked his connections and got in touch with *Vogue* magazine. Somehow he convinced the fashion magazine to give him a list of New York's hottest debutantes so that he could invite them to a "Torches of Freedom" demonstration. He pitched it as an event where the city's wealthiest young women would light up cigarettes at the annual Easter Day Parade, flaunting their liberation.

It was the perfect spectacle for the photo-hungry media, and the campaign was a roaring success. Women whose emotions were roused by thoughts of "freedom"—and by the sight of so many female influencers—started buying cigarettes and smoking them openly. As psychologist Lisa Held puts it, "Bernays was duly convinced that linking products to emotions could cause people to behave irrationally. In reality, of course, women were no freer for having taken up smoking, but linking smoking to women's rights fostered a feeling of independence."[2] In the wake of Bernays's success with the Lucky Strike campaign, advertisers began to study psychology to figure out ways to manipulate the unconscious minds of consumers. They would lure consumers in with emotional appeals or by associating a product with some political ideal like freedom.

Bernays's work was strongly influenced by progressive journalist Walter Lippmann, founder of the *New Republic* magazine, who had worked in the US propaganda office during World War I.[3] After his wartime experiences, Lippmann published a polemic called *Public Opinion*, in which he argued that democracy was being eroded by media manipulation and propaganda. Bernays's book *Crystallizing Public Opinion* was a sardonic tip of the hat to Lippmann's, whose ideas he cited while drawing the opposite conclusions. Bernays was thrilled by the power of media, and explained in step-by-step detail how intrepid public relations managers could use it effectively for advertising, corporate messaging, and political persuasion. Bernays described PR work as the "engineering of consent," and called it a new form of free speech. He wrote, "Freedom of speech . . . and [the] free press have tacitly expanded our Bill of Rights to include the right of persuasion."[4]

The truly creepy part? Bernays had successfully turned his

uncle's project to promote mental health into a system for manipulating people into behaving irrationally. Instead of helping people understand what they truly desired in their unconscious minds, he invited them to displace those desires onto something else, something they could buy. His Lucky Strike campaign channeled women's hopes for freedom into nicotine addiction. But Bernays always wanted to go beyond selling cigarettes. He believed that public relations campaigns could be done for countries just as easily as for corporations. Roughly twenty years after he got feminists hooked on smoking, Bernays used his media-manipulation skills to topple a nation's government.

Freud, again, provided an inspiration for Bernays's foray into international politics. In 1921, the psychoanalyst published a monograph called *Group Psychology and the Analysis of the Ego*, in which he suggested that humans had a "herd instinct" and could easily be led into irrational behavior by influencers. Though Freud imagined those influencers to be patriarchs—fathers, heads of state, religious leaders—Bernays realized that they could be anyone, from a debutante to a grubby newspaperman. Freud thought that the herd mentality was dangerous and could lead to political catastrophe. Lippmann, who feared its power over the free press, agreed. But Bernays embraced it.

At the dawn of the Cold War, Bernays was hired to run a campaign for United Fruit to popularize bananas in the United States. Most were from Guatemala, where the government allowed United Fruit (now Chiquita) to own 42 percent of the country's land, where it grew crops on vast plantations without paying local taxes. Bernays's plans to make bananas the number one American snack hit a snag when Guatemalans elected Jacobo Árbenz Guzmán (known popularly as Árbenz), a reformer who wanted to stop colonial-style exploitation, in 1951. Árbenz began to confiscate uncultivated plantation lands, including 210,000 acres belonging to United Fruit. He divided the plantations up into one hundred thousand plots and handed them over to impoverished Guatemalans. Árbenz also demanded higher wages for agricultural laborers. Bernays was outraged. His campaign to gin up demand for bananas was reaching a fever pitch, but his client was losing both land and money. While the United Fruit PR team continued to regale Americans with stories about the wonders of bananas, Bernays worked with the CIA to get his clients' plantations back.

Using his business connections, Bernays activated a network of spies in Guatemala to get intel on Árbenz's background and any connections he might have to the Soviet Union. According to Larry Tye, author of *The Father of Spin: Edward L. Bernays and the Birth of Public Relations*, Bernays claimed that a trustworthy source had told him that Guatemalan "Reds" were using weapons supplied by the Soviet embassy in Mexico City. He leaked intel like this to carefully selected journalists and soon the papers were full of rumors about Guatemalan communists plotting to take over the country. Colleagues in the United Fruit PR department found Bernays's tactics distasteful. Tye writes, "Thomas McCann, who in the 1950s was a young public relations official with United Fruit, wrote in his memoir that 'what the press would hear and see was carefully staged and regulated by the host. The plan represented a serious attempt to compromise objectivity.'" Still, Bernays's plot worked: thanks in large part to what he called a "scientific approach" to "counter-Communist propaganda," many people in the United States came to believe that Guatemala was a threat. Few journalists questioned why a small group of anti-Árbenz forces was able to stage a coup in 1954, overthrow Guatemala's democratically elected government, and hand thousands of small Guatemalan-owned farms back to United Fruit. In 1997, declassified documents revealed that the CIA had aided the men behind the coup with training and supplies— and their black ops were justified by stories about a communist threat, spread by a PR guy who wanted to sell bananas.[5]

To understand how psychological warfare developed in the United States, we need to keep in mind the bloody tale of Bernays and his banana propaganda.

THE BIBLE OF PSYWAR

When Paul Linebarger was writing *Psychological Warfare* for the US Army in the late 1940s, he was operating in the world that Bernays and Madison Avenue had made. Equally important, he benefited from a push within the Army to establish what became known as the Office of Psychological Warfare, headed by Brigadier General Robert McClure.[6] Before 1951, the military had had no ongoing units devoted exclusively to psyops—generally psywar units were brought together temporarily during periods of war, drawing personnel from different groups devoted to irregular warfare or information management. But as the Korean War heated up, Army leadership determined that these disparate efforts should be unified under McClure—and that psywar units would no longer be disbanded during peacetime.

Unlike McClure, Linebarger does not usually appear front and center in histories of Cold War psyops, and he preferred it that way. He was an academic and operative who worked behind the scenes, as much an observer of psywar as a practitioner of it. Perhaps that's why he was in the perfect position to write *Psychological Warfare*. It was one of the first military handbooks to codify a number of ad hoc practices for controlling large masses of people in order to win a war, using public relations and mass media. The book, originally a classified pamphlet made available to select Army personnel in 1948, became the first teaching manual for people working within McClure's newly organized psywar units. The influence of Linebarger's book during the Cold War spread outward from the Army and into the intelligence community at large. Journalist Scott Anderson, author of *The Quiet Americans: Four CIA Spies at the Dawn of the Cold War*,[7] describes how much the book meant to a young CIA agent named Rufus Phillips III. Phillips had joined a dozen other operatives for a new initiative described by their commander, Edward Lansdale, as "whatever we can do to save South Vietnam." It was 1954, and they had no idea what to do. But then Lansdale handed Phillips a copy of Linebarger's *Psychological Warfare*, which Phillips called the "bible on the topic." Reading that book was his only training. Within weeks, Phillips was designing crash courses in psyops for the South Vietnamese military.

Thanks in part to Linebarger's work, Cold War psyops came to resemble an advertising campaign backed up by violence. It was an approach he had first seen implemented during World War II. "The war we have just won was a peculiar kind of advertising campaign, designed to make the Germans and Japanese like us and our way of doing things," he wrote in *Psychological Warfare*. "They did not like us much, but we gave them alternatives far worse than liking us, so that they became peaceful."[8] Those "alternatives" included what his contemporaries called simply the Bomb.

The Bomb was the kinetic weapon that shaped the Cold War mindset. Everyone from American schoolkids to Soviet nuclear scientists had witnessed atomic bombs obliterating Hiroshima and Nagasaki, and now humanity was living with the reality of a weapon that had never existed before: one that could actually wipe out our species. The world's greatest nuclear powers, the United States and the Soviet Union, needed sneaky ways to attack each other without directly declaring a war that could cost them everything. Psyops were one way to do it. During this period, both nations established military and intelligence bureaucracies that waged an icy battle of ideologies. Their episodes of brinkmanship exploded into violence during the Korean War, the Vietnam War, and many other proxy battles throughout the world. But the superpowers' attacks on each other were counterbalanced by a profound fear of nuclear war. Cold War psychological warriors used that fear the way atomic weapons manufacturers used uranium.

Linebarger's work depended on the idea that psyops campaigns would always be overshadowed by the threat of nuclear annihilation. Directly after the bombing of Hiroshima and Nagasaki, as the horrors of those attacks were still unfolding, he worked with the US Army to create one of the most important influence campaigns of the war: the United States leaked the Japanese government's offer of surrender while the terms were still being negotiated. Linebarger described how the operation went down:

> The Japanese government pondered [the conditions of surrender], but while it pondered, B-29s carried leaflets to all parts of Japan, giving the text of the Japanese official offer to surrender. This act alone would have made it almost impossibly

difficult for the Japanese government to whip its people back into frenzy for suicidal prolongation of war.[9]

Linebarger believed this campaign worked partly because "so many people [were] being given so decisive a message, all at the same time." The mass dissemination of the message was as important as the message itself. To sway public opinion, US psywarriors needed the Japanese masses to understand that a surrender was in the works before the government could walk it back. As Linebarger wrote, the United States won largely because they "got in the last word."

Linebarger added his own peculiar expertise to the mix of psychology and public relations that defined twentieth-century propaganda. In his secret life as Cordwainer Smith, he was publishing some of the most acclaimed science fiction stories of the 1950s and '60s. He was brilliant at building imaginary worlds that felt so real that some of his readers were convinced the secretive author was a covert agent from a distant future. Literary critic Gary Wolfe, who has written extensively about Linebarger's fiction, told me that "so much is unexplained [in Smith's stories] that readers assumed the writer had forgotten to fill in background because he knew it to be true. People thought he was an actual time traveler."[10] It turned out to be the perfect skill for a propagandist.

PORTRAIT OF THE PSYWARRIOR AS A YOUNG NERD

Linebarger was born in 1913, on the eve of World War I. He was named after his father, Paul Myron Wentworth Linebarger, a lawyer and diplomat who was a close personal adviser to Sun Yat-sen, leader of the Chinese nationalist party Kuomintang. Sun became interim president of the Republic of China after ousting Emperor Puyi during the Xinhai Revolution of 1912, while the elder Linebarger worked as an operative for the Chinese nationalist government overseas. The two men were so close that Sun became the younger Linebarger's godfather, inspiring in the little boy a fierce anti-communism and lifelong loyalty to the Chinese nationalist movement. Growing up, Linebarger often traveled with his father across Asia and Europe, and at the age of thirteen wrote enthusiastically in his journal: "I love Shanghai. Paradise!!! I don't want to go away. Nothing on earth equal to this place. I don't want to go away. Never! Never!! Never!!!!!" The last two sentences were underlined, and the exclamation points got bigger and bigger until they ran off the page. In some ways, his feelings never changed. Linebarger spent his life fighting the communists who he believed were wrecking the beloved China of his childhood.

At the Hoover Institution Library & Archives, I pored over his childhood journals, which he kept assiduously from the time he was eleven through his early graduate school years. Bound in thick, cracked leather, each volume was a microcosm of the adult Linebarger would become. Tucked into the flower-printed endsheet of one journal were bits of ephemera: a page of Chinese characters he was practicing in his shaky hand, a photograph of himself with a group of Chinese dignitaries on a ship, and a picture of the Horsehead Nebula cut out of a science magazine. Another journal held a close-up photograph of the Moon; the edges had gone fuzzy, as if he'd carried it around in a pocket and taken it out frequently to look at. In the journals he kept as a kid, Linebarger wrote an index of their contents, which always included "stories of adventure" or science fiction alongside his studies in history and foreign languages. The older he got, the more he filled his journals with secret codes and stories, as well as love poems (mostly to his sweethearts, but once, memorably, to his Buick). Even as a tween, he had a sharp political eye, writing about the "impressive ceremony" he saw in the Capitol when President Calvin Coolidge took the oath of office.

What emerges from these bits of juvenilia is that Linebarger loved the feeling of traveling between worlds as an observer. In 1928, when he was fifteen or sixteen, he described a blissful trip to Chicago, where he visited Chinatown to pay his respects at the Kuomintang office on behalf of his father, then went to a bookstore to buy the latest *Amazing Stories Annual* and several Edgar Rice Burroughs novels from the Barsoom series that began with *A Princess of Mars*. From the very beginning, Linebarger's interests were equal parts practical and fantastical.

Linebarger earned a PhD in political science at Johns Hopkins University, specializing in Asian history, while also working for his father and the Kuomintang. By that time, he was fluent in many languages, including at least two dialects of Chinese. Sun Yat-sen gave him the name Lin Bai-lo, which he used when working in China. As Linebarger ascended the academic hierarchy, landing teaching jobs at Harvard and then Duke, he invented more names for himself: pseudonyms for publishing fiction. None of those pseudonyms is better known than Cordwainer Smith, whose admirers have included the powerful midcentury science fiction editor Frederik Pohl, author of a sharp satire of far-future admen called *The Space Merchants*, as well as literary stars like Michael Chabon and Ursula K. Le Guin. By the time Linebarger was working in the Office of War

Information (OWI) in 1942, he was using many aliases, all so that he could build worlds out of words.

President Franklin Delano Roosevelt used an executive order to create the OWI, which handled psyops and propaganda throughout World War II. Thanks to his familiarity with China, Linebarger was invited to join as a Far East specialist. It didn't hurt that he was also fluent in German, which made him a nimble analyst of Axis propaganda. OWI was modeled partly on the Committee on Public Information, an agency created during World War I, whose adept use of newspapers for propaganda had inspired Walter Lippmann's warnings in his book *Public Opinion*. Linebarger was thrilled to have a historical template for psyops that combined military interests with mass media. "Psychological warfare is good for everybody," Linebarger wrote enthusiastically, characterizing it as "the affirmation of the human community against the national divisions which are otherwise accepted in war."[11] This counterintuitive framing of propaganda as "affirmation of human community" fits neatly into a worldview where the only alternative to words is the Bomb.

"I MUST CRANCH!"

Linebarger believed that psyops should ideally be as appealing overseas as Hollywood movies were. He made fun of typical propaganda films for their clumsy patriotism and boring plotlines, and criticized them for failing to target international audiences. "Tahitians, Kansu men, Hindus and Portuguese would probably agree unanimously in preferring the USA of Laurel and Hardy to the USA of strong-faced men building dams and teaching better chicken-raising," he wrote.[12] Still, he didn't propose that future operatives make cleverer movies or more engagingly written propaganda. Instead, he offered suggestions for psyops that were, at first glance, more like dirty tricks than stories. If the adversary suffered from economic hardship in war, he wrote, the United States might "[drop] a few hundred tons of well-counterfeited currency" from planes. For "a country suffering from too much policing," one might make "facsimile personal-identity cards in large numbers." He continued: "The essence of this, as of all good black propaganda, is to confuse the enemy authorities while winning the thankfulness of the enemy people—preferably while building up the myth within the enemy country that large, well-organized groups of revolutionists are ready to end the war when their time comes."[13] Linebarger believed that effective psyops planted the seeds of stories, encouraging the enemy to create its own "myth" that resistance to the regime was already underway.

This is how Linebarger introduced science fiction into psyops. Immersed in the science fiction community, he was familiar with the idea of worldbuilding, a term popular among writers trying to create realistic fictional universes that are detailed and emotionally resonant enough to suspend an audience's disbelief. Good worldbuilding chips away at the audience's skepticism by providing plausible, consistent details. Think, for example, about why audiences are drawn to big franchises like Star Trek or Lord of the Rings. Both stories offer worlds that are rich with historical background, featuring complex political relationships alongside novel technologies and magical items. There are even specially constructed languages, like Klingon and Elvish, that fans can learn to speak. Notice that none of these worldbuilding details hinge on plot or character—they are consistent, believable sets and props that suggest many kinds of stories and myths, without being stories on their own. They are, in essence, a version of those black propaganda drops that Linebarger imagined would lead to mythmaking.

Linebarger wasn't the only sci-fi author who worked in intelligence, nor was he even the first. Rose Macaulay, who worked for the British Propaganda Department during World War I, published the novel *What Not* in 1919, a dark near-future satire about a fictional government propaganda agency called the Ministry of Brains. The Cold War brought more authors into the fold. Alice Sheldon, a CIA analyst in the 1950s, wrote secretly under the name James Tiptree Jr.; one of her most famous stories, "The Girl Who Was Plugged In," is about a future where corporations build remote-controlled cyborg influencers to become pop stars and shill products. Though Macaulay and Sheldon appeared to be conflicted about their propaganda work, some in the science fiction community were eager to join the war effort. Larry Niven, author of the 1970 novel *Ringworld* and many tales of interstellar war, consulted with the Defense Department in the 1980s on how to prepare for futuristic threats. John Campbell, influential editor of the magazine *Astounding Science Fiction*, wrote regular columns in the 1960s bashing communism and student protest movements; he urged his writers to take anti-communist positions in their stories too.[14] In the 1980s, organizations like the Global Business Network brought futurists and science fiction authors together with intelligence agencies to engage in "foresight" workshops, where the US government tried to game out possible threat scenarios.[15]

The overlap between the sci-fi community and psyops continues today. Ruth Emrys Gordon is a researcher who studies online disinformation for the government. Under the name Ruthanna

Emrys, she published *A Half-Built Garden*, which explores the future of social media after aliens make contact with Earth. What's notable about all these authors is that they rarely wrote stories intended to persuade an enemy to change their behavior. Despite editor Campbell's exhortations, they did not write psyops. Instead, they wrote about the process of *making* psyops, unfurling tales about controlling people's minds with media or other, more fantastical technologies.

Cordwainer Smith was no different. He built intricate future worlds in order to imagine what made people in them choose to rebel. Linebarger's first published story under the Smith moniker, "Scanners Live in Vain," plunges the reader into an alien-yet-familiar setting where Martel, the narrator, is stomping around his apartment, having a petty argument with his wife. At the same time, he's adjusting his blood flow, running diagnostics on his own body, and scanning his "chest box." Is this guy a human? A robot? An alien? All we know is that he has a very human wife, and she's listening to Martel blaring, "I tell you, I must cranch!" There's something uncanny about that word "cranch"—it feels like a term we should know, loaded with meaning, and yet it refers to nothing. It's a perfect example of worldbuilding: a tiny detail that sets our imaginations on fire.

As the story goes on, an entire military-industrial civilization slowly comes into focus behind what seems like a garden-variety marital spat. Martel, it turns out, is a "scanner," a half-biological, half-machine "haberman" whose body and mind have been optimized for interstellar travel by a vast imperial force called the Instrumentality of Mankind. He's undergone a horrific procedure that shuts down his entire sensorium so that he can survive the pain of space. When Martel uses a special wire to cranch, he temporarily regains the ability to use his five senses. Yearning to taste food and feel the touch of his wife's cheek again, he's become dangerously addicted to cranching—and it's making him question the political system. Martel agonizes over his life choices, and argues with his colleagues about how they're being used by the Instrumentality. Their minds are controlled, their morals attenuated. And then, as the story comes to a close, a rebellious scientist figures out a new technology to protect people during space flight. It turns out that "life" is a shield against the pain of space, and so the Instrumentality builds space vessels with shielding made of oyster beds. Now the oysters absorb the pain, and people like Martel no longer need to cranch. They can be human again, though we're left with the uneasy sense that millions of oysters will be tortured.

In many ways, "Scanners Live in Vain" is a fantasy about the bloody process of government reform. But it's also about how people can be controlled when they are systematically deprived of sensory input from the outside. The scanners are, in some sense, living deep inside a propaganda hole—only by cranching do they sense a way out. For Linebarger, a psyop should be like the cranching wire. At first, it's a pleasurable escape. Then it's a signpost on the road to revolution.

Linebarger wrote a whole sequence of Cordwainer Smith stories about rebellions against the Instrumentality, which eventually lead to a nominally more democratic "new age." Two of those stories, "The Dead Lady of Clown Town" and "The Ballad of Lost C'mell," deal explicitly with political uprisings bolstered by psyops. Both turn on the fate of the "Underpeople," nonhuman animals who have been mutated to perform menial labor for the near-immortal humans and cyborgs who rule the Instrumentality. In "The Dead Lady of Clown Town," a rebellious cyborg—the "dead lady" of the title—sparks a successful uprising among the Underpeople by forming a secret alliance with the dog girl D'Joan, a future revolutionary leader. This scenario is straight out of Linebarger's psyops playbook: our cyborg operative foments revolution against the government by finding allies within a disgruntled underclass. And in "The Ballad of Lost C'Mell," the revolution continues when a cat woman named C'Mell forms an intense telepathic bond with a lord of the Instrumentality, inspiring him to liberate the Underpeople. Telepathy, or mind-to-mind communication, was a major theme in Smith's work and in Cold War science fiction generally. It's easy to see why telepathy would become a widely used metaphor during a period where the world's great military powers fought to control people's thoughts.

Throughout the Underpeople stories, we see the theme of adversaries forming bonds that challenge an empire. As his Cold War colleagues in the Army worked covertly with anti-communist insurgents in Vietnam and Cuba, Linebarger imagined fantastical worlds where US psywar strategies actually worked. Though insurgents often lost in the real world, the Underpeople won. It was perhaps a form of wish fulfillment. Still, it was also a way for Linebarger to build scenarios for himself, to test ideas about psychological warfare in the sandbox of his imagination.

FASCIST INFLUENCERS OF THE RADIO AGE

To grasp a nation's propaganda strategies, Linebarger argued,[16] a student of psywar should choose one or two forms of media and monitor them for a lengthy period. Linebarger spent most of his research time listening to the radio, which was a crucial medium for psyops during World War II. Much like social media on the internet today, radio programming could be accessed at all hours with small, portable devices. Amateurs vied with professionals to rule the airwaves, which meant that twirling the dial could unleash commentary, music, or news from sources that were sometimes difficult to identify. As if anticipating the rise of platforms like Twitter and Facebook, propagandists would create fake broadcasts whose sole purpose was to deliver psyops. Nazi radio propaganda featured a chaotic, ever-changing set of commentators, including official government representatives alongside fake British news broadcasters pushing defeatist messages to demoralize English speakers. Germany created what Linebarger dubbed "falsified stations," such as one calling itself the New British Broadcasting Company, which a distracted listener might mistake for the actual BBC. Sometimes, the OWI analysts would discover "ghost programs" or "ghost voices" that would pop onto the Allied radio band when official programs went off the air.[17]

One of the fascists' great innovations was to create microcelebrities, or influencers, to attract listeners. A British defector named William Joyce became one of these influencers, joining the Nazi radio program *Germany Calling*, a broadcast that could reach English listeners across the sea with a medium-wave signal. Born in the United States to Irish parents, Joyce moved to England as a boy and spent his young adulthood working with British intelligence during the Irish War of Independence. After a brief stint in college, he devoted himself full-time to working as a political operative. In 1932 he joined the British Union of Fascists (BUF). Joyce chafed under the BUF's leader, Sir Oswald Mosley, whom he considered insufficiently antisemitic. Kicked out of the BUF in 1937, he formed the short-lived National Socialist League, a pro-Nazi organization that was focused on hatred of Jews.[18] Feeling that he couldn't fight for Britain, Joyce fled to Berlin in 1939 and was hired by the Nazis to write and broadcast fascist propaganda on a radio program that began with Joyce intoning, "Germany calling, Germany calling."

Using a plummy British accent and lacing his commentary with sarcastic jokes about the Allies, Joyce aimed his psyop straight at England. He took on the nickname "Lord Haw-Haw," which was coined by British radio critic Jonah Barrington (a pseudonym for Cyril Carr Dalmain) in an article about the broadcasts in the *Daily Express*: "He speaks English of the haw-haw, damn-it-get-out-of-my-way variety, and his strong suit is gentlemanly indignation."[19] Joyce urged other Allies to join the Nazi cause by trumpeting Germany's conquests in northern Europe, and snarking about how terrible life was in wartime Britain, with its food shortages. He parodied bad advice from what he called "the British Ministry of Misinformation."[20] Troops and civilians would tune in because Lord Haw-Haw had a charismatic personality and was sometimes the only source of news about troop movements during information blackouts. Of course, Lord Haw-Haw always exaggerated the number of war dead among the Allies, but he let just enough truth through the cracks to hook his listeners night after night. The British press tried to undermine Lord Haw-Haw's popularity by producing a series of newsreels in 1940 called *Nasti News from Lord Haw-Haw*, which often portrayed the commentator as a middle-aged gentleman with a monocle, occasionally held at gunpoint by a bumbling Nazi. In one film, the fake Haw-Haw proclaims that he's broadcasting "nothing like the truth" before making fun of the Germans for cooking soup out of old bathwater.

Needless to say, Joyce was nothing like the British newsreels portrayed him—he was a true believer in the Nazi regime, and joined Joseph Goebbels's propaganda team after a lifetime of supporting fascist causes. Captured in 1945, he was executed for treason. His moniker lived on, becoming synonymous with Nazi radio propaganda. In 1947, *Time* called Douglas Chandler "America's Lord Haw-Haw" after he was found guilty of treason for joining the Nazis and "spew[ing] forth the propaganda line of Joseph Goebbels" on the radio.[21]

The success of figures like Lord Haw-Haw led to another of Linebarger's important observations about propaganda: it is nearly always built on truth. Lord Haw-Haw was popular in England partly because he reported on the war at a time when most news was being censored by the British government. "It is the *purpose* that makes it propaganda, and not the truthfulness or untruthfulness of it," Linebarger wrote.[22] If a broadcaster uses truth to "affect the minds and emotions of a given group for a specific purpose," Linebarger argued, it is propaganda. And then, as if channeling the debate between journalist Lippmann and PR man Bernays, he concluded: "Opinion analysis pertains to what people think; propaganda analysis deals with what somebody is trying to make them think."[23]

Linebarger felt that one of the OWI's greatest accomplishments was the establishment of Voice of America, a radio station aimed at bringing a US perspective to the world. The OWI took over Voice of America in 1942, and programmed everything from popular music to carefully crafted bits of truth. Voice of America could be read as a real-life analog of the cranching wire from the Cordwainer Smith story "Scanners Live in Vain." Using their wire antennas to tune in, people deprived of information and entertainment could briefly experience the freedom that comes from both. Eventually, Linebarger hoped, the joy of cranching with Voice of America might lead to the reform of closed regimes like the People's Republic of China. Throughout the Cold War and beyond, adversaries could hear American voices whispering in their ears, almost as if they were sending telepathic messages about why democracy is good for the world.

Radio was Linebarger's medium of choice, but he also advocated using as many systems as possible for reaching the enemy. "Propaganda must use the language of the mother, the schoolteacher, the lover, the bully, the policeman, the actor, the ecclesiastic, the buddy, the newspaperman, all of them in turn," Linebarger argued.[24] Following the playbook laid out in *Psychological Warfare*, US operatives sought to tell the anti-communist story by speaking in many voices, partly through targeted operations and partly through a diffuse influence on the arts and science. Frances Stonor Saunders writes in *The Cultural Cold War* about how CIA money found its way into arts agencies that funded abstract expressionists like Jackson Pollock, whose splatterpaint style was deemed an affront to the Soviet realist aesthetic.[25] And Audra Wolfe's book *Freedom's Laboratory* reveals how the CIA funded an outreach campaign to Chinese scientists, hoping to turn them into US sympathizers.[26]

Still, the vast majority of psyops were not fancy products carefully designed to seduce enemies into siding with America. They were the same kinds of leaflet-and-loudspeaker operations that went all the way back to World War I. Billions of propaganda leaflets were deployed alongside kinetic weapons in the Korean War, Vietnam, and other hot spots.[27] Yet even these bog-standard paper bombs, as leaflet drops were often called, were not held in high regard by military leadership. According to military historian Mark Jacobson, "When forced to choose between leaflets, loudspeakers and firepower [during the Korean War], operational leaders chose firepower."[28] Compounding this problem was the difficulty measuring whether a psyop had worked. It's not as if soldiers could go out into the field and count how many people within a five-mile radius of a paper bomb had been persuaded to embrace American ideology. Linebarger and his colleagues wanted to tempt their adversaries with promises of hope and freedom, but the reality was that most leaflets were full of basic threats or news intended to hurt morale. Violence and intimidation remained the military's favorite forms of persuasion.

Lurking behind the gunfire and loudspeakers was the greatest threat of all: the Bomb. Even though it was the world's most powerful kinetic weapon, the Bomb was also one of the greatest psyops of the Cold War. Never deployed after Hiroshima and Nagasaki, but always hovering in the background, it was a source of fear, paranoia, and lingering unease even during peacetime. Kids prepared for nuclear attack by learning to "duck and cover" in their classrooms. Adults read journalist John Hersey's 1946 book, *Hiroshima*, a series of harrowing eyewitness accounts from survivors of the Bomb. It was impossible to forget that any moment could be humanity's last.

In his fiction, Linebarger reflected on the deep connection between psychological war and the Bomb. His story "Mother Hitton's Littul Kittons" introduces us to a mysterious device that the

Instrumentality uses to protect Earth's resources from their many enemies. The weapon is essentially a psychological atom bomb, made by a group of scientists who have bred the most vicious, insane, bloodthirsty minks in the world. Thousands of these mutated minks are kept asleep in a special facility—if they wake up, they will rip one another apart—and their minds are attached to a telepathic amplification device that can deliver their collective consciousness into space. When an interloper tries to steal Earth's supply of stroon, a life-extending drug, the Instrumentality's forces awaken the minks, and their thoughts are "ground into [the thief's] brain." First "the synapses of his brain re-formed to conjure up might-have-beens, terrible things that never happened to any man." Then, he "screeched with animal lust as he tried to devour himself . . . not entirely without success." Having pulled out his own eyeballs and eaten his arms, the intruder dies from the results of a telepathic assault from thousands of angry weaponized minks. Bonkers and yet utterly horrifying, the story is also a fascinating metaphor for psychological operations. The enemy destroys himself, without any damage to anyone else, through a kind of radical demoralization. This is perhaps Linebarger's most emotionally realistic representation of typical psyops, which aim to hurt rather than seduce.

I spoke to Linebarger's daughter Rosana Hart about how he explained his work to her, and she told me about a memorable conversation she had with her father. "I asked why some people have hard lives and other people don't," she recalled. "He basically said that's how it is. It was like he was trying to explain the world to me. I think he felt it was his job to explain how the world works, [through] pain and tragedy. In Mexico, he would tell us about the cruelty of Spanish to the Mexicans and the Indigenous. He would go into more detail about suffering than a child should have had to listen to." She paused, and then sighed. "He wanted me to know that danger was there."

THE BRAINWASHED GENERATION

As psychological war became established military doctrine, rumors began to circulate that communists fighting in the Korean War had even more powerful mind-control methods than the United States did. Fittingly, the origin of these rumors is shrouded in conspiracy theories even today. In 1950, a staunchly anti-communist journalist named Edward Hunter published an article in the *Miami Daily News* called "Brain Washing Tactics Force Chinese into Ranks of Communist Party." Hunter covered news from Asia, and claimed that "Mao's Red Army" used a reeducation tactic called *xi-nao*, which literally translates to "wash brain."[29] According to Hunter, *xi-nao* was a play on words, a reference to the Confucian idea of *xi-xin*, meaning "to wash the heart, a metaphor [for preparing] oneself for a quiet retirement from world affairs."[30] People subjected to brainwashing, Hunter explained in his article, became like robots, easily programmed to do whatever their captors asked. Some even turned against their own allies. Hunter's implication was that there could be brainwashed sleeper agents anywhere in the world, just waiting for the right moment to strike.

His idea caught fire in 1950s America, where the Bomb had already primed people for paranoia. Hunter's ambiguous relationship with the CIA—which he touted frequently—added spice to the tale by making it seem as if he, too, might be some kind of spy with insider knowledge. At least one reporter in Hong Kong, Tillman Durdin, said that Hunter worked directly for the CIA and reported to Joseph McCarthy about other reporters he suspected of having communist sympathies.[31]

A more likely story is that Hunter used these rumors of CIA involvement to boost his reputation and sell books. It turned out that the *Miami Daily News* story was a teaser for a book that Hunter published in 1951 called *Brain-Washing in Red China: The Calculated Destruction of Men's Minds.* The book was packed with stories about Korean War veterans who described a form of mental torture they'd experienced in Chinese POW camps. During years of imprisonment, these men were subjected to terrifying indoctrination sessions and long periods of social isolation, often standing outside in the freezing wind without shoes. The prison guards' goal seemed to be converting POWs into propagandists who would go on the radio to spread communist ideas to their fellow Americans, sort of like an earnest version of Lord Haw-Haw. Former POWs who exhibited classic symptoms of PTSD—apathy, nightmares, inability to focus, hypervigilance—were said to be suffering the aftereffects of brainwashing. Though many experts have disputed that Chinese troops were actually using the term "brainwashing," it became a powerful meme in the United States. Hunter jealously guarded his role as the man who coined the term. He raged at *Time* magazine's editors for writing about brainwashing in 1951 without crediting his book, sending countless letters to colleagues and his publisher asking them to put pressure on the magazine to acknowledge that he had introduced the term "brainwashing" to the world.[32]

There's no disputing that Hunter popularized the word, but Linebarger probably wrote about it first. Ten days before Hunter's

Miami Daily News story, historian Marcia Holmes writes, Line-barger sent a technical memo to his colleagues in the intelligence community where he described "an endless process which is called by the nick-name of 'brainwashing,'" used by communist interrogators on Korean and Chinese people.[33] It seems likely that brain-washing was being discussed in military circles before it hit the mainstream press.

Dutch psychoanalyst Joost A. M. Meerloo added a new element to the idea of brainwashing in his 1956 book, *The Rape of the Mind: The Psychology of Thought Control, Menticide, and Brainwashing*. He believed that the modern obsession with technology, especially television, was akin to Pavlovian conditioning, priming people to become obedient mechanisms themselves. He was one of the first commentators to notice that television was replacing radio as the medium of choice for propaganda, though his rather extreme argument was that television was inherently totalitarian, a hypnotic device that turned viewers into compliant automatons. Meerloo believed that "mechanization was the cause as well as the effect of brainwashing," as University of Groningen social scientist Maarten Derksen puts it.[34] It was, Derksen adds, a dystopian view that fed into increasingly science-fictional notions of what exactly psyops could accomplish.

Very quickly, brainwashing came unmoored from its original context and took on a much broader meaning. Anyone might be brainwashed, especially if they took an interest in the countercul-ture or civil rights movements. In the late 1950s, E. Merrill Root published *Brain Washing in the High Schools*, in which he blamed US soldiers' vulnerability to brainwashing in Korea on supposedly Marxist teachings in American high schools. And FBI director

J. Edgar Hoover talked about the dangers of communist "thought control" in his book *Masters of Deceit: The Story of Communism in America and How to Fight It*. Calling somebody "brainwashed" in the 1950s and '60s was like invoking the "woke mind virus" in the 2020s—it implied that leftists had planted dangerous ideas in Americans' vulnerable minds, causing previously good citizens to question their nation's greatness. As Harvard science historian Rebecca Lemov writes, "Brainwashing became a nation's shared concern, a creeping worry all could viscerally understand, so that the power of the idea extended well beyond the contexts in which it was originally envisioned to operate."[35]

That said, there were plenty of hippies who described establishment types as "brainwashed" too. Basically anyone who didn't share your point of view could potentially be a brainwashed dupe of some suspicious authority. Starting in the 1950s, there was also a subgenre of popular science writing that purported to explain all the ways Americans were being brainwashed by the advertising industry and Hollywood. Vance Packard argued in his 1957 bestseller *The Hidden Persuaders* that advertisers were actively trying to induce neuroses in consumers, to get them emotionally hooked on buying everything from cars to cigarettes. He'd revealed what the military's psyops groups had known for half a century: advertising is a great model for propaganda.

A fear of brainwashing haunted pop culture too. Science fiction movies like *Invasion of the Body Snatchers* (1956) depicted an alien menace that converted Americans into emotionless, brainwashed automatons. In 1962, Frank Sinatra starred in a dark thriller called *The Manchurian Candidate*, which followed a group of POWs coming home from Korea. Sinatra's character starts having weird hallucinations, and eventually we realize—shocker!—that the communists have turned him into a mind-controlled assassin. Philip K. Dick, author of *Minority Report* and *Do Androids Dream of Electric Sheep?* (which was adapted into the movie *Blade Runner*), wrote many stories about the twin threats of psyops and advertising; in his novel *A Scanner Darkly*, for example, the main character is hired by the government to spy on himself, after a drug splits his mind into two personalities.

The question of how to resist brainwashing was also on everyone's mind. Some, like Vance Packard, sought to educate the public about how they were being manipulated. Others, such as L. Ron Hubbard, the sci-fi author turned cult leader, promised to free people from brainwashing—by offering them a *different* kind of brainwashing. Hubbard launched the Church of Scientology after the success of his 1950 bestseller, *Dianetics*, a mishmash of New Age beliefs and science fiction tropes presented as a way to reject psychological manipulation. Readers learned how to clear the "engrams," or damaging memories, from their minds in order to become fully actualized. The rituals of Dianetics, codified into religion as Scientology, were intended to reassure people that their minds were free of alien influences. Linebarger was fascinated by Hubbard's work (though not a true believer), as evidenced by his unpublished book "Ethical Dianetics,"[36] about how Dianetics could be viewed as an effort to popularize psychology among ordinary people.

Though supposedly brainwashing was a weapon used only by US adversaries, the CIA nevertheless dabbled in its own brainwashing program, called MK-Ultra, a well-funded series of experiments aimed at turning mind control into a legitimate social science. Historian Rebecca Lemov writes that at its peak, the MK-Ultra program cost taxpayers almost a billion dollars per year, and funded everyone from behaviorist B. F. Skinner, who experimented with conditioning animals in his "Skinner Boxes," to famed anthropologist Margaret Mead. One of the CIA's front operations, called the Human Ecology Fund, gave money to people who wanted to investigate whether it was possible to control people by controlling their environment.[37] There are dozens of books and even a movie, *The Men Who Stare at Goats* (2009), about the sensational experiments the CIA and Army conducted using LSD, hoping that the hallucinogen might become a foolproof truth serum (it didn't). The paranoia around mind control became so self-justifying that one is forced to wonder whether Edward Hunter's popularization of the term "brainwashing" was its own kind of meta-psyop, intended to rationalize the CIA's expensive anti-communist antics.

It's the kind of neurotic musing one might have after reading a Cordwainer Smith story or Philip K. Dick novel. At the height of the Cold War, psyops held a contradictory position in the public mind: on one hand, they were associated with the terrifying myth of brainwashing where humans became robots, while on the other, they were a sought-after specialty in legitimate military and policy circles. A whole new field had grown out of psychology, public relations, advertising, and storytelling. Wedded to the military-industrial complex and the Bomb, it was a powerful weapon. Put another way, battlefield subterfuge became an office job, and its practitioners normalized the process of threatening people in the name of democratic freedom. At the same time, psyops were associated with fantastical ideas like brainwashing and Scientology's engrams, which meant Americans were never sure what to believe about the mind-control powers their government really had.

As radio and television programming saturated the nation's cultural imaginary, people asked increasingly urgent questions about what was real and what was propaganda. Media critic Marshall McLuhan published an influential essay collection in 1964, *Understanding Media*, where he asserted that technologies like television and computers had created an entirely new psychological environment. War, he wrote, was now "an electric battle of information and images that goes far deeper and is more obsessional than the old hot wars of industrial hardware."[38] He was right about the "electric" part. But the American battle over information and images goes back to the nation's earliest days.

CHAPTER 2

A FAKE FRONTIER

A s Master Sun's millennia-old work *The Art of War* attests, psywar has deep historical roots. To understand the US approach to psyops—a fusion of threats, fictions, and Madison Avenue hucksterism—we have to investigate its past. That means going back further than World War I and the Office of War Information, to the dirty, chaotic wars between US militias and hundreds of Indigenous nations during the nineteenth century. The Indian Wars were a period of violent mythmaking, where the United States used everything from schoolroom lessons to adventure novels to justify the nation's bloody westward expansion. Many of the psychological weapons developed during the Indian Wars became prototypes for the professional psyops products deployed during the twentieth century and beyond. We cannot fully grasp the nation's specific brand of psyops without journeying back in time over 240 years, to witness how it all began.

Benjamin Franklin pioneered one of the first American psychological operations during the Revolutionary War. This was during the most violent years of the conflict, when Britain did not recognize the United States as a nation, and settler militias were using guerrilla tactics to push the British out of North America. To grow their fighting forces, the settlers allied with their Indigenous neighbors, including the Oneida and Tuscarora Nations. The British did the same, allying with the Seneca tribe among others. Franklin wasn't a soldier, but he had something more powerful than a musket: a printing press. In 1782, he created a fake newspaper[1] that he hoped would undermine the British public's faith in their government's tactics. Franklin gave the paper a realistically bland name, *Supplement to the Boston Independent Chronicle.*[2] All the articles in the *Supplement* were written by Franklin himself and printed in his own shop. Mostly, he wrote horrifying descriptions of the ways innocent Americans suffered under British occupation, conjured in fabricated "eyewitness accounts" of battlefield mayhem and mutilation.

One article in particular went viral, eighteenth-century style. Franklin wrote it under the name of a made-up militia officer, who claimed the British were ordering Seneca troops to kill and scalp US soldiers, settlers, and children. This nonexistent officer described seeing hundreds of scalps being sent from British officers "as a Present to Col. Haldimand, Governor of Canada, in order to be by him transmitted to England." Full of gory details about the boxes of tattered scalps, the tall tale made a splash overseas. A British newspaper, the *London General Advertiser and Morning Intelligencer*, reprinted the fake story in full. Then the story took off in the United States, where dozens of papers, in New Jersey, New

York, Rhode Island, Connecticut, and Pennsylvania,[3] cited the London *General Advertiser*'s account as their source for the false claim that Britain's Seneca allies were scalping US farmers and children. Franklin's ploy had worked. He helped sour British people on what their rulers were doing in North America. And he did it by throwing Seneca soldiers under the bus, fomenting hatred between US settlers and Indigenous people.

In 1794, as the Revolutionary War ground to a close, soldiers from the United States fought the British for the last time. The two sides clashed on a tornado-ravaged section of the Maumee River where shattered trees were strewn along the banks. Dubbed the Battle of Fallen Timbers, it's remembered as the last skirmish of the Revolutionary War, where US forces quickly beat back their adversaries and took control of land that eventually became the state of Ohio. Except it wasn't fought by American and British troops alone; the British had enlisted allies among the Chippewas, Wyandots, and members of other federated tribes. The Battle of Fallen Timbers was a harbinger of many wars to come between Indigenous nations and the United States. It signaled the start of an ideological war against Indigenous ways of life, complete with proto-psyops, brainwashing, and propaganda aimed at rewriting the history of North America. It was also the beginning of organized Indigenous resistance to colonization. Toward the end of the nineteenth century, western tribes launched counter-psyops that became models for future protest movements against the US government.

The Indian Wars have no set beginning or end. From the seventeenth century through the late nineteenth century, US leaders pushed the nascent country's borders west in a series of chaotic, bloody battles that left at least a million people dead.[4] Some chroniclers call these conflicts the Frontier Wars, but I'm following the lead of Yale historian Ned Blackhawk, author of *Violence over the Land: Indians and Empires in the Early American West*, who calls them the Indian Wars.[5] That is what combatants called them at the time, which is worth knowing. More importantly, this name acknowledges that these wars were waged by the US government against Indigenous nations and tribes, rather than for the liberation of an abstract "frontier."

Franklin's anti-Indigenous propaganda in the *Supplement* didn't come out of nowhere. It was based on an even older tradition of demonizing the enemy that dated back to King Philip's War in the 1670s. This was a particularly devastating battle between New England colonies and the Wampanoag tribe, in which tens of thousands of people died and many Wampanoag survivors were enslaved.[6] After the war was over, a false narrative took hold in settler communities. New Englanders claimed that their triumph in King Philip's War meant that Indigenous tribes had "died out" in their region of the country. Scholars call this the "myth of the vanishing Indian."[7] It was propaganda aimed primarily at white settlers, to justify the wars and enlist the aid of Europeans living in Indian Country. And it was a story that people still told a century later, at the height of the Indian Wars.

Like a lot of propaganda, this myth was internally contradictory. It's a matter of public record that the US War Department appropriated millions of dollars[8] to fight the Indian Wars in the nineteenth century. If the enemy had already vanished, leaving a virgin land for whites to settle, why the need for all that funding? Still, liberal East Coast settlers preferred to believe that the United States had a legitimate claim to western lands because Indigenous people were, as one anthropologist put it, "culturally extinct."[9] The idea was that tribes had naturally faded away as their members assimilated into European society, becoming Americans instead of Wampanoags, Mohicans, or Oneidas. One of the most popular books in the United States during the 1820s was James Fenimore Cooper's *The Last of the Mohicans*, which Cooper claimed was an accurate historical account of how quickly European settlers had wiped out tribes in the Northeast. This would have been news to the Mohican people who were alive when the book came out and to their descendants living on tribal land in Wisconsin today.[10] Not to mention members of all the other tribes who survived alongside them. And yet the myth of the vanishing Indian put down deep roots, shaping both military strategy and white settlers' perception of Indigenous people.

It was a very seductive psyop, perpetuated by the US government, military, and pop culture. European settlement was recast as an inevitable process of population replacement, in which Indigenous nations were naturally erased by the spreading borders of the United States of America.

INVENTING THE WILD WEST

Frontiers are not natural. On the landmass known today as North America, the wild frontier was a legal fiction intended to make it easier for the United States to win the Indian Wars. It was named in the 1834 Indian Trade and Intercourse Act, where the US government established what it called the "permanent frontier," or "permanent Indian frontier." The "frontier" referred to lands west of the Mississippi River that would be left to the Indigenous groups who lived there—either because it was their home or because they had been relocated there by force. The War Department built a series of forts along that frontier, stretching from Fort Snelling in Minnesota to Fort Jesup in Louisiana. Soldiers stationed along the frontier had two mandates: protect white settlers living on Indigenous lands, and prevent the tribes from warring with one another.[11]

Kori Schake, a former policy adviser with the Department of Defense, compares the Indian Wars to the twenty-first-century US occupation of Afghanistan. She highlights, in particular, how unready US soldiers were, and how little communication passed between groups. "Soldiers fighting successive tribes of Indians ... were mostly militia, with little prior experience of warfare," she writes. "The army did not carry lessons from one Indian War over into the next." Militias were mustered and disbanded all over the United States, all with slightly different mandates and economic support. As a result, it was almost impossible for the federal government to enact any specific policy, and local officials made little effort to honor promises and treaties the federal government had made with tribes. Militia commanders often had no knowledge of a given tribe's legal status. In both the Indian Wars and Afghanistan,

> [there was an] unwillingness by political leaders to acknowledge the scope and contradictory nature of their strategic objectives; an enormous gap between the campaign's objectives and the resources political leaders are willing to put toward the effort; dramatic overestimation of the capacity of our government to effectively carry out a sophisticated policy with political, economic, and military elements;

corruption delegitimizing the idealistic components of the policy designed to win support of "reconcileables"; ... insularity in Washington against the consequences of the policy's failures, which are principally borne by others; [and] a military hesitant to credit their adversaries with superior tactics and even strategy.[12]

Rarely do we hear experts describe the Indian Wars in these terms. It's widely acknowledged that the Afghanistan occupation was monstrously complex and riddled with problems that went right to the top. And yet when the Indian Wars are evoked, they're reduced to a simplistic tale of US soldiers versus tribes on the wild frontier. Schake's account is far more accurate.

The first major wave of military conflict came just a few years before the frontier was born, sparked by an event referred to euphemistically by the US government as "removal." For the Seminole, Choctaw, Chickasaw, Cherokee, and Creek Nations—sometimes called the Five Civilized Tribes—it was known as the Trail of Tears. After President Andrew Jackson signed the Indian Removal Act in 1830, he appropriated $500,000 (roughly $15.6 million today) to clear Indigenous groups out of the southeastern territories claimed by the United States. It was the first of many payouts for this purpose. Though the act didn't explicitly direct the president to deploy the military—indeed, it was framed as a peaceful "land exchange"[13]—it did give him permission to "remove" all the sovereign tribes from their land in "exchange" for land on the Oklahoma frontier. The act also called for the US government to provision them with "support and subsistence" for a year after their resettlement, and to protect them from "interruption or disturbance" from other tribes and individuals. This is a key point, often forgotten, largely because the government provided almost nothing other than a cold, hard road to Oklahoma.

In the two decades following passage of the Indian Removal Act, the federal government forced tribe after tribe off their lands, using a combination of military muscle and legal threats. The result was a refugee crisis of epic proportions, with poorly provisioned Indigenous families marching hundreds of miles to Oklahoma—sometimes in freezing weather. Alexis de Tocqueville, the French diplomat who celebrated American freedom in his book *Democracy in America*, was an eyewitness to the removal of the Choctaw Nation. He described thousands of people dying of starvation and exposure during the journey. At one point, he wrote, desperate Choctaw families left their dogs behind so they could cross a freezing river on rafts; the crying dogs plunged in after them, fighting the icy currents. The sight of families ripped apart, losing each other and their lands, filled him with foreboding. "These are great evils; and it must be added that they appear to me to be irremediable," de Tocqueville wrote, adding that he feared the tribes would be completely eradicated.[14]

They were not. When members of the Choctaw Nation arrived in Oklahoma, they suffered further from disease and malnutrition. They had lived their whole lives in the tropics, after all, and initially they were ill-equipped to make a home on the cold, dry plains. Still, they survived; there has yet to be a "last Choctaw." The US government made a few haphazard efforts to protect the newly relocated tribes, allocating money in dribs and drabs. In 1832, after two years of conflict over the Indian Removal Act, Congress gave $20,000 to the Stokes Commission,[15] a group of men led by former North Carolina governor Montfort Stokes, to improve Indigenous life. But the commission spent all its time working with the War Department to coerce western nations including the Comanche, Kiowa, Wichita, and Osage into ceding territory to newly relocated tribes from the Southeast. Clearly, there was nothing peaceful about the "land exchange" described so blandly in the act. American militias fought the tribes, the tribes fought one another, and US government bureaucrats argued bitterly over what should be done.

Indigenous nations tried several strategies for resisting the Indian Removal Act. In Florida, the Seminole military responded with force, winning battles with US militias for decades. Others tried to beat the settler government at its bureaucratic game, by using the legal system. Cherokee chief John Ross sued the state of Georgia twice in an effort to prevent tribal lands in Georgia from being confiscated and sold off to white settlers. The first case was brought by the nation and the second by a group of sympathetic white missionaries, led by Samuel Worcester, who were living on Cherokee land.[16] The Supreme Court heard both cases, and in 1832 the Justices ruled in *Worcester v. Georgia* that the state did not have the right to remove the Cherokees.[17] "The Cherokee Nation, then, is a distinct community occupying its own territory . . . in which the laws of Georgia can have no force," wrote Chief Justice John Marshall in the decision. President Jackson sneered at the ruling, turning a blind eye as the state of Georgia continued to sell off Cherokee land. Within a few years, federal troops finished the job by forcing the Cherokees off their remaining land in Georgia.

Given the very public nature of the Indian Wars, and the horrors of the Trail of Tears reported by Indigenous and European eyewitnesses, you'd think it would have been hard to pretend that the Western frontier was wild and empty. It was *obviously* full of people—so many, in fact, that it required millions of dollars in federal spending to clear them off. And yet, all across New England, settlers set about convincing themselves that Indigenous nations were fading away. They did it, according to University of Minnesota historian Jean O'Brien, in the most boring way possible.

YET ANOTHER "LAST INDIAN" STORY

O'Brien was a history graduate student at the University of Minnesota when she stumbled across an odd little book of roughly 140 pages, full of poems, historical addresses, hymns, and a cringey description of an Indian impersonator's antics onstage. It was an amateur town history, published to commemorate the bicentennial of Bridgewater, Massachusetts, in 1856. "It was hilarious," O'Brien recalled with an infectious laugh. She was speaking to me by video from the hotel where she had just arrived for a history conference. "The funniest part was when they talked about [buying land] from Massasoit and from Ousamequin. But they're the same person." She paused to shake her head ruefully. "They probably had no idea. There's confusion because they're telling a false narrative." Back when she first laid eyes on the Bridgewater document, O'Brien wasn't sure what that false narrative was—she simply knew "it didn't add up." It wasn't just because the people of Bridgewater didn't know that Massasoit and Ousamequin were both names for the seventeenth-century Wampanoag chief. It was also the fact that someone at the bicentennial gave a speech mourning the fact that all the Indians their ancestors encountered in the region had disappeared. "It really caught my attention," she said, because it mirrored myths of the "last Indian." A member of the Ojibwe tribe from Minnesota, O'Brien didn't have firsthand knowledge of what had happened to New England nations, but she was certain these histories were part of a dark cultural pattern that was all too familiar. She wondered how many "last" stories she could find. "I was searching for what I thought of as the smoking gun. Could I find 'last' stories that contradicted themselves?"

O'Brien's curiosity sent her down a very long research hole, which eventually landed her at the American Antiquarian Society in Worcester, Massachusetts. She discovered that the Bridgewater centennial document was one of hundreds of amateur histories published by local New England historical societies in the mid-nineteenth century. She tore through them, spending every day in the library for nine months. "When I told my friends they thought I was crazy because [these histories] are deadly boring. They are so bad." She grinned. But, she recalled, she found the smoking gun—more than one, in fact. Nearly every book, pamphlet, and oration she read about small New England town history shared a common trope: each began by mourning the loss of the "last Indians," while also celebrating the first European settlers. And then, seemingly without realizing that they were contradicting themselves, authors would describe Indigenous families living currently in their towns. O'Brien told me she found this pattern over and over in her research: town histories would describe people from local tribes as extinct and alive at the same time. "I thought they were hilarious," O'Brien told me. Eventually she published a book about her findings, *Firsting and Lasting: Writing Indians out of Existence in New England.*

At the time they were published in the nineteenth century, these local histories were not laughable. In fact, O'Brien told me, they were taken quite seriously. People read them voraciously, and not just in New England. One of the first historical pamphlets O'Brien found, a local history from Connecticut, had once been in the personal collection of the University of Minnesota's president. "Can you imagine that?" she asked. It would be like a university professor today using sunny tourism brochures as a source of historical facts about an area. Amateur histories featuring "last Indians" were sponsored by local governments to make their towns sound important, and in their often stultifying prose they revealed how many white Americans had internalized the myth that Indians disappeared after the early northeastern wars.

O'Brien was careful to point out that some historians did not play the propaganda game. Frances Caulkins, author of several Connecticut histories, acknowledged the ongoing existence of many tribes. Her contemporaries, however, leaned into the "last Indian" myth by defining Indigenous identity in a very narrow way. For example, many amateur historians did not consider Indians who converted to Christianity to be Indian anymore. The same went for Indians who became US citizens and for Indians of mixed heritage. In fact, settlers didn't seem to view anyone as Indian unless they wore traditional garb, spoke their native languages, and lived the way their ancestors had two hundred years before. As O'Brien put it, Indigenous people were defined as the opposite of modern. For Europeans to acknowledge them as Indians, they needed to conform to an outdated stereotype of "primitive" hunter-gatherers. It would be like insisting that a modern-day Londoner wasn't truly British unless they spoke in Shakespearean English, wore a giant ruffled collar, and traveled across the sea by galleon. And yet that was exactly what these settlers demanded of their Indigenous neighbors.

An Indigenous person who used modern technologies, or who had adopted aspects of European culture, was not a "true Indian" according to settlers. That was the flawed logic settlers used to convince themselves that Wampanoags, Mohicans, and other Indigenous people in New England had gone extinct. O'Brien pointed out that this idea still affects public policy in the United States. "When you have fishing rights disputes, for example, the anti-sovereignty angle starts with, 'Well, you're not fishing the way you used to, so why should that be protected as a treaty right? Take that motor off your boat,'" O'Brien said. "That's part of the whole 'Indians can never be modern' idea." One of the implicit messages of those nineteenth-century amateur histories was that Indigenous sovereignty had no future. By erasing the existence of their Indian neighbors, these historians were suggesting that Indigenous cultures would never exist again. It was a double erasure, with political implications that could appeal to both conservative and liberal voters in the United States.

Conservatives were eager for any evidence that Indigenous nations were fading out of existence. President Jackson and other politicians in the 1830s had made treaties with the nations to provision them with supplies and protection. When voters didn't believe that Indians were, in fact, Indians, it was easy for government representatives to duck out of their treaties by claiming that the nations named in them had been converted or assimilated. Liberal New Englanders had a different concern. O'Brien told me that local historians often wanted to put some distance between New England's relationships with Indigenous nations and the brutal Indian

Wars taking place in the Southeast and West. She noted that many New England histories begin by describing town founders making legitimate land deals with local tribes, who then conveniently went extinct. Because so many New England voters in the nineteenth century were opposed to Jackson's removal policies, amateur historians wanted to reassure readers that their own town founders were nothing like the Jacksonian politicians raising militias to attack Seminoles and Cherokees.

New England town histories were shared stories that retold American history by, as O'Brien put it, "writing Indians out of existence." Social scientists call this phenomenon historical amnesia.[18] Groups often experience a kind of collective forgetting about horrific events like genocide and war, especially because most people would prefer to stop thinking about them.[19] Emotional storytelling, whether fictional or factual, is one way to draw a curtain of amnesia over historical events, transforming the way we look back on our past. Studies have shown that people can forget details of traumatic events they've lived through when they listen to persuasive stories about those events from other people.[20] As O'Brien discovered in her research, even a stultifying local history can be emotionally powerful. For settlers who wanted the Indian Wars to be over, these amateur histories offered soothing half-truths that absolved them of guilt. In the mid-nineteenth century, it would have been deeply calming for settlers to read that Indigenous nations were disappearing on their own. That meant they could forget about the war.

While the military tried to wipe out Indigenous people in kinetic wars, there was a parallel cultural assault happening in those pamphlets that O'Brien's friends called boring. During nice New England historical society tea parties and town square festivities, settlers were telling stories about how terribly sad it was that the Indians were gone. It was a convenient way to forget about the treatment of actually existing Indigenous tribes all across North America. Amateur histories and novels like *The Last of the Mohicans* touched on a genuine truth—nations were being decimated—but twisted it to suggest the Indian Wars and forced relocations were not to blame. As Bernays might have observed, it was propaganda that helped to sell white settlers on real estate in the West.

THE ORIGINAL BRAINWASHING PROGRAM

While the government pushed "last Indian" propaganda on voters, other psyops were aimed at Indigenous people. The goal in these operations was to make western nations surrender, and force their citizens to accept US culture as their own.

After the United States won the Mexican-American War in 1848—with a great deal of unacknowledged help from Comanche and Apache troops, who had been fighting the Spanish for years[21]—a new phase of the Indian Wars began. Today it's often called the "manifest destiny" period, though at the time there was nothing manifest or obvious about what the future of the United States would look like. The permanent frontier outlined in the Indian Trade and Intercourse Act grew porous and impermanent as the US government sought to expand its territories to the west, in Indian Country. Americans continued to squabble over whether that was a profitable or ethical idea.

The 1850s were a period of radical, progressive thought in the United States, partly inspired by the growing abolitionist movement. Frederick Douglass worked on antislavery legislation and addressed sold-out crowds at conventions. Under a pseudonym, Harriet Jacobs was writing articles and her classic memoir, *Incidents in the Life of a Slave Girl*. Countercultural white writer Nathaniel Hawthorne published his best-selling novel *The Scarlet Letter*, which explicitly criticized American moralism. Harriet Beecher Stowe's abolitionist tearjerker, *Uncle Tom's Cabin*, was another smash-hit book at the time, though Stowe's racist depictions of Black characters were part of what sold it to the white public. Still, many influencers of this period were questioning the nation's treatment of enslaved African Americans, which in turn sparked public conversation in the press and political debate over the treatment of Indigenous people in the West.

The progressive cultural turn of the mid-nineteenth century provoked strong conservative backlash. After California joined the union in 1850, its governor, Peter Burnett, delivered a State of the State speech that summed up a position taken by many political leaders in the West. "That a war of extermination will continue to be waged between the races until the Indian race becomes extinct must be expected," he proclaimed.[22] It was basically a mandate for white settlers to kill Indians, and thousands were murdered without legal repercussions.[23] By the time the United States was embroiled in Reconstruction, most of the clashes between Indigenous nations and settlers took place on the western plains and Pacific coast.

White progressives of the later nineteenth century took up the cause of Indigenous rights the way their parents' generation had taken up abolitionism, which is to say with equal doses of reformist zeal and polite racist cluelessness. Wealthy easterners formed groups like the Indian Rights Association, a charitable group that issued reports on the abysmal conditions on many Indian reservations and advocated for better treatment from the US government. The organization's members published a newsletter called *The Indian's Friend*, but their idea of friendship was to "civilize" Indians by Christianizing them, teaching them to farm using European methods, and forcing them to abandon their traditional community structures. They were continuing the project of denying Indians futurity, as historian O'Brien put it.

The question these reformers kept asking was how they could convince their Indigenous "friends" to assimilate peacefully and become Americans. In 1883, wealthy philanthropist Albert K. Smiley decided to figure it out. He invited some of the nation's most prominent reform-minded men to his posh lodge in Lake Mohonk, New York. Politicians, high-ranking military officers, missionaries, and people we would today call thought leaders joined Smiley at what the *New York Times* dubbed in 1892 "the Lake Mohonk Indian Conference."[24] No Indians were invited. The Lake Mohonk conferences convened annually for three decades, and their wealthy, connected attendees shaped policies that changed how the government dealt with tribes well into the twentieth century.

Nearly all those policies centered on education. Lake Mohonk liberals wanted to "uplift" Indigenous children by teaching them English and Christianity, and training them for jobs as farmers or other skilled laborers in European settlements. To nineteenth-century white philanthropists, it sounded like the height of enlightened policy. But the reality was terrifying. The US Army took Indigenous children away from their families and enrolled them in residential schools that were often hundreds of miles away, making visits and communication impossible. Parents and children might not see each other again for years—if ever. Perhaps these schools weren't conceived as an explicit form of brainwashing by Smiley and his Lake Mohonk buddies. But US politicians made it clear that Indian boarding schools were a form of conquest, a companion to kinetic war. As historian David Wallace Adams explains in his history of residential schools, *Education for Extinction*,[25] that's exactly how Secretary of the Interior Carl Schurz framed it in 1882. "[His] argument was that it was less expensive to educate Indians than to kill them," Adams writes. "[Schurz] estimated that it cost nearly a million dollars to kill an Indian in warfare, whereas it cost only $1,200 to give an Indian child eight years of schooling." As Edward Hunter might have put it in his books about brainwashing, it was a form of ideological indoctrination. The government wanted to turn Indigenous kids from many nations into adults who truly believed in European cultural values and would spread those values in their communities until there were no more Indians.

Funding for residential schools had begun in 1819, when the US Congress passed the Civilization Fund Act, which allocated money for introducing the "arts of civilization" to tribes near white settlements. Initially, the government partnered with missionaries to set up schools, but in 1824 the Bureau of Indian Affairs was established to run programs for "civilizing" Indigenous people.[26] That meant the US government was firmly in the driver's seat, often assigning the same officials to oversee Indian wars and Indian schooling.[27] But it wasn't until the influence of the Mohonk conferences and other organizations that congressional funding for residential schools exploded, jumping from $20,000 in 1877 to $1.4 million in 1890.[28] Politicians touted these schools as a humane way of turning Indigenous people into proper citizens of the United States. But as many survivors of the system pointed out, residential school was traumatizing, destroying family connections and extinguishing tribal cultures.[29] The damage was not exclusively psychological, either. In 2022, US Secretary of the Interior Deb Haaland released a series of reports on how children in these schools were abused, neglected, and sometimes murdered by the people who were supposedly civilizing them.[30] Like POW camps, Indigenous boarding schools were full of violence and abuse. They were nineteenth-century brainwashing machines, institutions that forced kids to accept the ideology and morals of a nation that was at war with their own. It's no wonder that Americans so quickly embraced the myth of Chinese brainwashing during the Korean War. The United States had already practiced it against adversaries a century before.

GHOST DANCE MORAL PANIC

Battered by armies and educators, nations in the West responded by embracing a revolutionary movement that honored Indigenous cultures of the past, and looked forward to a future after the white settlers were gone. It was called the Ghost Dance.[31]

In the late 1880s, around the time when the Lake Mohonk gang was advocating for a dramatic expansion of the residential school system, a Paiute man named Wovoka had a vision. He said that the Creator had come to him with a new dance, one that would bring about a better world without white settlers and their endless expansionist wars. The dead would reunite with the living, and the buffalo killed by settlers would roam the plains again.[32] It's not difficult to understand why this message would be profoundly moving for people who had lost so much in the Indian Wars and whose children were being taken away for reeducation by the US government. It was a story about a hopeful future, where Indigenous culture flourished and the land came back to its original caretakers. Oceti Sakowin (Great Sioux Nation) historian Nick Estes, author of *Our History Is the Future*, writes that the government had outlawed Indigenous dancing at that time, and therefore "the Ghost Dance was fundamentally oppositional in spirit."[33]

John Fire Lame Deer, a Lakota man whose grandfather Lame Deer was in the Battle of the Little Bighorn, recalled hearing about the Ghost Dance from his elders. He told journalist Richard Erdoes that Short Bull and Kicking Bear "became leaders of the ghost dance." He continued:

> They told the people that they could dance a new world into being. There would be landslides, and earthquakes and big winds. Hills would pile up on each other. The earth would roll up like a carpet with all the white man's ugly things—the stinking new animals, sheep and pigs, the fences, the telegraph poles, the mines and factories. Underneath would be the wonderful old-new world as it had been before the white fat-takers came.[34]

Estes explains that word about the Ghost Dance spread like wildfire through residential schools, where students "transcribed Kicking Bear's and Short Bull's reports [in English and Lakota] after the two men traveled by train to meet with Wovoka."[35] People performed the dance in large groups, often wearing sacred Ghost Dance regalia covered in pictures of animals, the sun, and the moon. Within months, the practice had spread across the plains, taken up by the Sioux, Cheyenne, and Arapaho Nations, among others—all of whom added their own ideas about what the Ghost Dance meant and how it should be performed. The dance was both a spiritual revival and a protest movement, combining traditional Indigenous beliefs with tactics of resistance that included opposing reservation authorities, refusing to speak English, avoiding church, and preventing children from going to residential schools.[36] The Ghost Dance provided a strong counterpoint to the messages emanating from educators and policymakers. Dancers celebrated the Indigenous civilization that had existed for centuries before white settlers arrived, participating in a tradition of social-movement building that went back at least as far as the Mississippian urban complexes of the 900s. Cahokia, a thousand-year-old city at the fork of the Missouri and Mississippi Rivers in southern Illinois, was founded in the midst of a similar kind of movement that took the plains by storm.

White settlers and the US military responded to the Ghost Dance with what can only be called a moral panic. Newspaper reports from 1890 referred to the dance as something weird and terrifying, with headlines like "Heap a Big Scare," "Ghost Dance Mania," and "That Messiah Craze."[37] It was mistakenly called a war dance, a prelude to aggression. Government anthropologist James Mooney and General Nelson Miles, a prominent figure in the Indian Wars, pushed back on these stories, explaining that the Ghost Dance was peaceful.[38] But rumors began to spread that the dance was a sign of imminent attack on nearby white settlements. Fears about the ritual were at their height in late 1890, when Lakota war hero Chief Sitting Bull allowed a group to perform the Ghost Dance at his camp on the Standing Rock Reservation. In response, the US government dispatched 100 members of the cavalry and ordered tribal police to arrest Sitting Bull on a cold day in December. When the police arrived at Sitting Bull's house, the chief resisted arrest and roughly 150 of his followers gathered outside his home to protest. According to Mooney, who interviewed Indigenous eyewitnesses, one of the protesters shot a police officer, Bull Head, who responded by shooting Sitting Bull.[39] Another police officer on the scene, Red Tomahawk, shot Sitting Bull in the head and killed him instantly. Though this altercation was the result of military and police violence, the Ghost Dance was blamed. Even forty years later, in Red Tomahawk's 1931 obituary, the *New York Times* framed the incident as "the tribe ghost dancing preparatory to revolt against the white man."[40]

Witnesses said otherwise. And the events that came after, known as the Wounded Knee Massacre, suggest that the US military was using the Ghost Dance as an excuse to kill bands of Lakotas. After the police shot Sitting Bull, his band fled the area with his elderly brother Spotted Elk, hoping to find safety on the nearby Pine Ridge Reservation. For over a month, US cavalry units had been massing around Pine Ridge, spurring thousands of Indigenous people living there to flee into the freezing winter badlands of South Dakota. Two weeks after Sitting Bull's murder, the Army surrounded his band where they were camped near Wounded Knee Creek. US soldiers ordered the Lakota warriors to surrender their guns, and began searching through the band's tipis, making threatening comments about what they would do once everyone had been disarmed. When one of the warriors refused to give up his gun, the cavalry opened fire on the Lakota men, whom the US soldiers had separated from the women and children. Fearing for their lives, the women fled into a ravine, where the cavalry systematically hunted them down and killed them. Eyewitnesses from both the US and Lakota sides[41] testified that the Army murdered unarmed people, including a pregnant woman waving a flag of surrender. When the shooting stopped, US soldiers told the remaining survivors— mostly young boys—that they would be spared if they came out of hiding. When the children did, they too were shot. In all, about three hundred members of Sitting Bull's band died that day, some of whom were babies and children who died of exposure after their mothers were killed.

In the days that followed, a few lucky survivors and residents of the Pine Ridge Reservation came to the scene of the massacre to witness what had happened and gather up mementos from the dead. Estes writes that armed Lakota men continued to resist the military in the badlands, and a young residential school victim named Plenty Horses shot and killed a US soldier. Brought up on charges of murder, Plenty Horses was acquitted in a key ruling that determined the entire Wounded Knee Massacre had been conducted during a state of war.[42] That meant the soldiers who shot Sitting Bull's band were innocent as well. The ruling painted both the massacre and Indigenous political movements as military attacks, making it appear that both sides were aggressors and equally culpable. It was a kind of psyop on the part of the court, framing the massacre as simply a lost battle in the Indian Wars—and yet another piece of evidence that Lakota citizens were dying out.

SITTING BULL, WILD WEST SUPERSTAR

News about the Ghost Dance and the Wounded Knee Massacre spread around the world, thanks to an unexpected source: Wild

West shows, live-action reenactments of the Indian Wars. We know that the Ghost Dance was staged in those shows partly thanks to Sam Maddra, an intrepid researcher at the University of Glasgow Archives in Scotland, who worked with a group of Wounded Knee descendants to repatriate a Ghost Dance shirt that had somehow made its way to Scotland in the 1890s. The story of that shirt's strange journey reveals another side to Chief Sitting Bull, and his efforts to establish Lakota sovereignty.

Sitting Bull wasn't just a Lakota war leader—he was a global celebrity, a symbol of the American West. Thanks to his friend William F. "Buffalo Bill" Cody, another famous figure from the Indian Wars, Sitting Bull briefly starred in one of Buffalo Bill's Wild West shows.[43] Wild West shows were in some ways the nineteenth-century version of reality TV, full of people reenacting famous battles. Many performers were former soldiers playing themselves. Some would do rodeo-like stunts on horseback or pseudo-educational programs about history. Audiences would come to big arenas, where Wild West shows were staged, to gawk at the stunts, meet war celebrities, and see battles that they had only read about. Buffalo Bill's Wild West show was one of the most successful, and Cody often employed Indigenous performers to play themselves in the mock wars. As Maddra explains in her book *Hostiles? The Lakota Ghost Dance and Buffalo Bill's Wild West*, joining the show was one of the few ways that Indigenous men could get work off the reservations.[44]

In 1885, Sitting Bull toured with Cody's show. Unlike most Indigenous performers, Sitting Bull did not "play Indian" in one of the war reenactments. Instead, he was introduced with appropriate fanfare for a war hero and made a dignified circuit around the arena on horseback. Sometimes he would give a short speech through a translator. These appearances electrified audiences and no doubt sowed the seeds for the bizarre pop cultural turn that the Ghost Dance took after the Wounded Knee Massacre.

After the massacre, the US government cracked down on Lakota citizens, confining them to reservations. But Cody hired nearly seventy-five men from Pine Ridge and nearby reservations for a European tour—twenty-three of whom, like Short Bull, were imprisoned leaders of the Ghost Dance movement. Maddra writes, "It is perhaps one of the greatest ironies of American Indian resistance, that the last Lakota to have forcibly resisted the government of the US were released into Cody's care where they proceeded to act the very 'roles' ascribed to them a year earlier."[45] Springing these men from jail may have been Cody's attempt to support the Lakota prisoners, but mostly it was a way to exploit their notoriety to sell tickets. Writing in *Hostiles?*, Maddra gives us a picture of how the Wild West show framed the Lakota performers for UK audiences:

> The Indians were presented by Buffalo Bill's Wild West as resolute barriers to civilisation; "a counter-force against which the hero displayed his virtues." This image was easily recognisable to a British public well-versed in imperialist propaganda. The notoriety of the Ghost Dancers was used to pull in the crowds, but except for their being introduced as the "Hostiles" as opposed to the "Friendlies," their role within the arena remained the same as the other Indian performers. The 1891–92 tour of Britain also included a "Wounded Knee orphan" who they presented as "the last of the stock," reinforcing the idea of American Indians as a vanishing race. The

young boy had survived the massacre and travelled with his adoptive parents No Neck and his wife Ellen.[46]

Western historian Patricia Limerick, author of *Something in the Soil*, put it another way: "The war turned colorful, quaint, and marketable in an amazingly short time."[47]

And this is where the Ghost Dance shirt comes in. After the Buffalo Bill show toured Scotland in 1891, a white member of the troupe donated an authentic Ghost Dance shirt to the Glasgow Museums, explaining that it had been taken from a person slain at Wounded Knee. And there it sat in the archives for over a century, until a visiting Cherokee lawyer saw the shirt in an exhibition and advocated for its repatriation.[48] Maddra, who was researching the history of the Wild West show in Glasgow, became an ally in the process, testifying before the Glasgow city council and eventually traveling to South Dakota for the repatriation ceremony.[49]

The story of that single Ghost Dance shirt, its journey to Scotland and back, tells us a lot about what the Ghost Dance meant to global audiences. Ghost Dancing began as a protest, an Indigenous vision of a world without white settlers. This was a powerful message when the dominant vision—taught to Indigenous children in residential schools—was of a world where white settler culture eradicated tribal traditions. The dance was a sharp rebuke to the "last Indian" narrative, showing that Indigenous culture wasn't dying out but was instead changing to meet new conditions. Considered in that light, it's no surprise that the movement was used by the US military to justify a violent crackdown. It was a cultural threat. Where it could not be contained by military might or government bans against Indigenous dancing, it was converted into reality entertainment by Buffalo Bill's Wild West show, which was playing into the "last Indian" myth that O'Brien found in history books. The Ghost Dance was at the center of a psychological war over the Indigenous future. Sitting Bull, Short Bull, and other Indigenous leaders aimed to secure a future where sovereignty meant retaining tribal traditions. White "friends of the Indian" like the Lake Mohonk crowd envisioned a twentieth-century America where Natives were entirely assimilated, their cultures relegated to graves and badly researched histories.

The Indian Wars took place at a time when nobody had any idea whether the West could be "won." And yet, by the early twentieth century, most Americans accepted the idea that "manifest destiny" had been the guiding principle of the Indian Wars, suggesting that the US government had always been steadfast in its commitment to owning the West. That's because the final psychological battle of the Indian Wars hinged on the question of how the nineteenth century would be remembered.

THE FIRST WHITE REPLACEMENT THEORY

The idea of "manifest destiny" became popular in the late 1880s to describe western expansion, but its origins were a lot more humble than that. Indeed, the phrase had been wrested so far out of its original context that it wasn't until the late 1920s that a University of Buffalo historian named Julius Pratt figured out where it had come from. "Manifest destiny" originated as part of an op-ed written in 1845 by right-wing newspaper editor John L. O'Sullivan for the *Democratic Review*. O'Sullivan was not writing about America's destiny to take the West; instead he was focused specifically on the annexation of Texas, arguing that it was the nation's destiny to take the contested territory from Mexico. Far from being a "true prophet of U.S. expansion," O'Sullivan was just a two-bit hack who quickly lost his newspaper job and went on to work as a propagandist for the Confederacy before becoming a spiritualist who claimed he could speak with the dead.[50]

Though O'Sullivan died in obscurity, the phrase "manifest destiny" was taken up by public figures; it was used by politicians advocating for the annexation of Oregon[51] and by the poet Walt Whitman, singing the praises of his expanding nation.[52] More importantly, it was ensconced in history books for decades, affecting the perceptions of generations of young Americans. This latter feat was thanks largely to a Harvard historian named Frederick Jackson Turner, whose "frontier thesis" is what popularized the idea of manifest destiny. The young professor presented his frontier thesis in a famous speech during the 1893 Columbian Exposition in Chicago. There he told the assembled crowd that westward expansion defined the American character. This was a departure from the assertions of thinkers in previous generations, including Alexis de Tocqueville, who thought of New England as the center of gravity in the United States. Instead, Turner argued, the western frontier was what forged a uniquely American identity. It was a place where settlers could reinvent themselves, shedding their European origins and constraining Old World traditions.[53]

Turner described the frontier in pseudoscientific terms, as a kind of rapidly evolving ecosystem where European settlers encountered Indigenous people and learned from them, then quickly overwhelmed and supplanted them:

The buffalo trail became the Indian trail, and this became the trader's "trace"; the trails widened into roads, and the roads into turnpikes, and these in turn were transformed into railroads. . . . The trading posts reached by these trails were on the sites of Indian villages which had been placed in positions suggested by nature; and these trading posts, situated so as to command the water systems of the country, have grown into such cities as Albany, Pittsburg, Detroit, Chicago, St. Louis, Council Bluffs, and Kansas City. Thus civilization in America has followed the arteries made by geology, pouring an ever richer tide through them, until at last the slender paths of aboriginal intercourse have been broadened and interwoven into the complex mazes of modern commercial lines; the wilderness has been interpenetrated by lines of civilization growing ever more numerous. It is like the steady growth of a complex nervous system for the originally simple, inert continent.

Turner argued that American identity was forged when white settlers replaced "Indian villages" with "cities," and converted "aboriginal intercourse" into "the complex mazes of modern commercial lines." His point was that the United States' foundational moment of statehood was not the Revolutionary War but instead the Indian Wars. That's when white settlers replaced western Indigenous communities with their own, and turned Indian land into commercially exploitable resources. Put another way, Turner was suggesting that Europeans became American in the nineteenth century by replacing Indigenous people. The frontier thesis was the original racial replacement theory. And the settler public loved it. Turner's "frontier thesis" idea was as popular at the turn of the twentieth century as Malcolm Gladwell's "tipping point" was at the turn of the twenty-first, sparking conversations among Americans in academia and on the streets.

It's not that there were no detractors. In fact, a decade before Turner's speech, a novelist named Helen Hunt Jackson published a scathing indictment of the US government's treatment of Indigenous people called *A Century of Dishonor*.[54] Using government documents and firsthand accounts from Indigenous activists, Jackson detailed several massacres of tribal bands as well as the many broken treaties that had promised land, supplies, and government representation. Unfortunately, her solution looked a lot like what the "friends of the Indian" suggested at the Lake Mohonk conferences: "civilizing" the Indigenous population through education and assimilation. Still, her work made it clear that many Americans didn't buy the idea that racial replacement was the nation's manifest destiny. As Jackson argued, there were hundreds of thousands of Indians still alive in the nation, and they deserved their rights as outlined in hundreds of treaties.

When her book was largely ignored, Jackson followed it up with an *Uncle Tom's Cabin*–style novel about the tragic life of a mixed-race Indigenous-Mexican girl, called *Ramona*.[55] Set in Southern California, it revealed the racism against Indigenous people on the frontier, where US culture clashed with the old ways of the Mexican Californios and many Indigenous tribes. Needless to say, the "good Indian" characters in *Ramona* are all Christian, and Jackson's subversive message about Indigenous rights—such as it was—was so faint as to be unrecognizable. *Ramona* became an instant bestseller, and was adapted into several movies in the first half of the twentieth century. D. W. Griffith, famous for his racist epic *The Birth of a Nation*, made a short film based on *Ramona* in 1910. The story became a romantic myth rather than an indictment of the United States' shameful policies and violence against Indigenous tribes.

If Turner's and Jackson's work represented two approaches to the psychological war that boiled alongside the Indian Wars, it's clear that Turner's approach proved the most popular. His vision of white settlers replacing Indigenous nations shaped how subsequent generations understood the nineteenth century—and how white settlers remembered (or, more accurately, failed to remember) Indigenous civilizations. On the other side of the psychological war, the one represented by Sitting Bull as a Lakota chief and celebrity, was the power of the Ghost Dance as a form of direct action. As historian Nick Estes points out, the legacy of the Ghost Dance continues in the present day, inspiring resistance movements like NoDAPL, where Lakota citizens and their allies clashed with the US government over plans for the Dakota Access Pipeline.

Though World War I was the first time that psychological war was identified as such, the practice of combining propaganda and mythmaking with total war began with the Indian Wars. The aftermath of the Indian Wars cast a long shadow across America's future. Over the next century, the psychological weapons developed during the nineteenth century were honed in the forge of World War I and produced at scale during World War II. Eventually, weaponized storytelling became so normalized in the social media era of the 2010s that it was hard to identify battlegrounds until it was too late.

CHAPTER 3

ADVERTISEMENTS FOR DISENFRANCHISEMENT

The United States is in the midst of a psychological war over voting. Every election cycle, whether for a local school board or the presidency, spawns hundreds of news stories about election misinformation online. A flurry of questions follows. Who is responsible for the misinformation? How should we respond to it? Does debunking a story about election fraud actually work, or does it entrench conspiracies more deeply in the American imagination? The only thing that seems certain, at this point, is that each election unleashes a barrage of lies, accusations, and manipulation from an unknown number of groups, whose aims seem opaque at best.

Social media election psyops have an unexpected origin story. In 1943, a group of three researchers from the University of California at Berkeley invented a new kind of personality test that they administered to thousands of Americans. They called it the F-Scale Test.[1] Put simply, this test could measure a person's likelihood of becoming a fascist. Else Frenkel-Brunswik, a Jewish psychiatrist who had fled the Nazis across Poland and Austria before finding a home in the United States, was still reeling from the meteoric rise of fascist leaders before World War II. She wanted to know how formerly peaceful people could send their neighbors, colleagues, and friends into death camps. Terrified that authoritarianism would spread throughout the world, she began working with her UC Berkeley colleague R. Nevitt Stanford and student Daniel Levinson on a single burning question: Was there a way to predict who would become a fascist, based on their personality traits? They took inspiration from tests used during World War I to measure soldiers' vulnerability to "shell shock," or PTSD, and devised a questionnaire intended to suss out people's latent political tendencies. What they found, after years of running the F-Scale Test, was that certain people do have a measurable disposition that primes them to follow strongman leaders with racist and antisemitic tendencies.

The three researchers collaborated with philosopher Theodor Adorno, who had fled Nazi Germany, to publish a book in 1950 called *The Authoritarian Personality*. In it, they broke down the psyches of latent fascists. People with "authoritarian personalities" were often cynical about humanity: they believed the strong would always rule the weak and that force was the only way to resolve conflicts. Authoritarians also had deep ethnocentric feelings that led to hatred of all manner of people unlike themselves: Jews, immigrants, homosexuals, political adversaries. They had a strong mistrust of science, which they associated with too much rapid social change. The higher a person scored on the F-Scale, the more likely they would fall for fascist propaganda. And yet, as Frenkel-Brunswik and her colleagues discovered, people with authoritarian leanings often didn't realize it. UC Berkeley intellectual historian Martin Jay, who has studied Adorno's work, told me that the book's "basic intuition" is that "people have surface beliefs but if you dig down they have psychological limitations that take them away from those beliefs. There are differences between conscious and unconscious motives—which explains why people would betray their ideals." A person might see herself as kindhearted, but clever anti-immigrant propaganda would get her thinking that "those people" are criminals who should be forced into detention camps. When triggered by rapid social changes, those unconscious beliefs could erupt into full-blown genocidal movements.

What Frenkel-Brunswik and her co-authors had uncovered was something that psyops experts already knew well, thanks to studying the advertising industry. Appealing to people's buried biases is the best way to activate them, for profit or for war. This created a new problem, at least if you wanted to prevent authoritarianism from spreading. As Jay put it, "The way to confront fascism wasn't at the level of argumentation. You had to confront unconscious motivations. So how do you deal with something you can't argue people out of?" The *Authoritarian Personality* research team had no answer to that question, but they had hunches. Educational reform was high on the list. They found that children who were taught without violent discipline were less likely to develop authoritarian personalities, and that early exposure to diverse people could ease ethnocentric aggression. If ordinary people could be turned into Nazis with the wrong prompting, perhaps the right prompting could reverse the process. Frenkel-Brunswik and her colleagues' goal, similar to the goals of many social media researchers today, was to protect vulnerable people from being exploited by fascists. Unfortunately, that's hard to do, especially when every generation invents a new system for emotional exploitation.

Over sixty years after *The Authoritarian Personality* came out, a very different group of researchers administered a personality test to hundreds of thousands of people online. Their test contained elements of the F-Scale, which is no surprise—the researchers, from a firm called Cambridge Analytica, were also trying to find latent authoritarians. Except they did it for the opposite reason that Frenkel-Brunswik and her colleagues did. The Cambridge Analytica team was helping authoritarian politicians target people whose minds were vulnerable to fascist propaganda. Christopher Wylie, research director at the firm, eventually became a whistleblower in 2018 and revealed the extent of his former employers' involvement with a massive operation to influence American voters in the 2014 midterms and 2016 presidential election.[2] Steve Bannon, one of Donald Trump's closest advisers, was a major player in Cambridge Analytica. Wylie explained his group's work to *The Guardian* as building "Steve Bannon's psychological warfare mindfuck tool."[3]

Cambridge Analytica was owned by a British company called Strategic Communication Laboratories Group (SCL), whose founder, Nigel Oakes, started his career in advertising and quickly moved into foreign-influence operations during the 1990s, working with British and US intelligence in Nigeria, Indonesia,[4] Libya, Syria, and Iran.[5] Seeking to branch out into electoral politics in 2013, the company hired young Canadian data scientist Wylie, who was in London working on a PhD in fashion forecasting. In addition to his marketing background, Wylie had experience with targeted political messaging from working on Barack Obama's 2008 presidential campaign. He quickly set to work creating what he told friends would be "the NSA's wet dream,"[6] a system that could create psychological profiles of American voters and target them for political manipulation. Soon after he started, Wylie met with Bannon, who then introduced him to right-wing billionaires Robert and Rebekah Mercer. Between 2013 and 2017, the Mercers pumped millions of dollars into Cambridge Analytica, while Rebekah and Bannon held positions on its board. Their goal, according to Wylie, was to fundamentally change American culture. "Rules don't matter for them. For them, this is a war, and it's all fair," Wylie told the *New York Times*.[7]

The "psychological warfare mindfuck" started in earnest in 2014, when Bannon and the Mercers asked Cambridge Analytica to create a tool that could, as Wylie put it in his memoir, *Mindf*ck*, "quantify society inside a computer, optimize that system, and then replicate that optimization outside the computer." All of that optimization hinged on electing the Mercers' favorite Republicans, like Senators Thom Tillis and Ted Cruz, who would dismantle the government and support big business. Bannon wanted something more, though. He told Wylie that a revolution was coming and its vanguard would be white people who "felt oppressed by political correctness."[8] Wylie was under intense pressure to produce an algorithm that could locate this vanguard online and activate their latent racial biases. He needed personality profile data, and he needed it fast. Seeking help, Wylie turned to a University of Cambridge psychology professor, Aleksandr Kogan, who was familiar with research showing that you could cobble together personality profiles based on people's "likes" on Facebook. Working with colleagues, they created a personality-test app that would run on Facebook, harvesting data about potential voters. The app was actually a test within a test—one people consented to take, and one they did not. The first test was based on a very common personality test called the Big Five. It rates subjects on—you guessed it—five personality traits:[9] openness, conscientiousness, extraversion, agreeableness, and neuroticism. Cambridge Analytica paid subjects on the gig-work platform MTurk a few dollars to spend about twenty minutes installing the app on Facebook and taking the test.[10]

As these unsuspecting MTurk workers on Facebook clicked through the Big Five test, Wylie and Kogan were also running a different test—the *real* test that would reveal who these people were. They planned to get their answers from sneakily procured Facebook profile data: age, sex, location, and likes. Exploiting a little-known Facebook policy that allowed academic researchers to harvest personal information from users,[11] Wylie and Kogan used the test app to siphon profile data from everyone who took the Big Five test. They also hoovered up profile data from friends of people who took the test on Facebook. It was this last bit—their ability to snarf up data from friend lists—that gave them the dataset of the NSA's wet dreams. Though only about 270,000 people took the app test, Cambridge Analytica was able to grab personal information from 87 million accounts. Wylie and Kogan believed this profile data could reveal Americans' secret desires and latent tendencies—especially the little thumbs-up icons that signaled engagement with topics from immigration and guns to LGBT rights and Black Lives Matter. Knowing people's likes and dislikes would make them ripe for manipulation, as long as the right political messages were crafted to trigger them.

Bannon was interested in reaching people who exhibited what psychologists call the "dark triad" of antisocial personality traits: narcissism, Machiavellianism (manipulativeness), and psychopathy (lack of care for others). People who score high on dark triad tests tend to be authoritarians who are willing to break the law to get what they want.[12] Using the tranche of ill-gotten Facebook data, Cambridge Analytica researchers trained an algorithm to predict who had the dark triad, based on their profiles. They targeted those people with ads, luring them to Facebook pages that the firm had set up to test out which messages worked best on these easily activated people. In his book, Wylie claimed that some of those messages included "drain the swamp" and "make America great again," which later became slogans of Trump's 2016 presidential campaign. Once a group of people with dark triad personalities had converged on a message, Cambridge Analytica operatives would encourage them to gather in a local bar or coffee shop, where they could swap conspiracy theories and strengthen their ties.

According to Wylie, Bannon believed that there were Democrats who were secretly racist, and all they needed was the proper nudge to be "deprogrammed" and brought over to the far right. Bannon tasked Cambridge Analytica with "identifying a series of cognitive biases that . . . would interact with latent racial bias." The firm began by targeting groups who felt "oppressed by political correctness." After a lot of testing, they hit on a message that got a powerful response: they asked subjects to "imagine an America where you can't pronounce anyone's name," then showed them a series of non-Western names and asked, "Can you recall a time where people were laughing at someone who messed up an ethnic name? Do some people use political correctness to make others feel dumb or get ahead?" By arousing people's sense of humiliation in an everyday situation—trying to pronounce an unfamiliar name—they hit a nerve. Once they had hooked people with this message, they escalated, feeding them stories about how "minorities were to blame for socioeconomic disparities between races," because they were inherently inferior to whites.[13]

The firm's strategy seemed to be working. After Wylie left the organization, Bannon put Cambridge Analytica to work on Trump's 2016 presidential campaign. Now it was time to deploy all the tools and messages they'd developed by manipulating people on Facebook who never knew they had shared their feelings with a group of political operatives. According to campaign officials, the firm was involved with "designing target audiences for digital ads and fundraising appeals, modeling voter turnout, buying $5 million in television ads and determining where Mr. Trump should travel to best drum up support." They were using Cambridge Analytica's millions of Facebook profiles, acquired without consent, to seek out voters who were vulnerable to what Frenkel-Brunswik and her colleagues would have called "authoritarian" messages about immigration and guns.[14] Internal correspondence at the firm revealed that they were also running a "voter disengagement" initiative aimed at African Americans, with the goal of confusing and disempowering a voting bloc that threatened Republican candidates.[15] Trump won that election and Bannon mobilized a new political force in America: the right-wing extremist internet.

It was another success for Cambridge Analytica, with far-reaching implications. By then, Wylie was working for the Canadian government—but was still haunted by the "nightmare" of Bannon's political strategy.[16] A few months later, he went public with the explosive information about how Trump's closest adviser and campaign funders were covertly attempting to wage psychological war on US citizens.

THE NEW RULES OF PSYOP

If the Cambridge Analytica story sounds like a strange twist in the history of US psyops, it is. It goes against basic psychological operations training in the military. I know this from experience, because I took a crash course in what the Army refers to as PSYOP. (Though it's not an acronym, the military loves an all-caps spelling.) My instructor taught PSYOP in the US Army for many years, and to protect his identity, I'm calling him Han Solo. Irascible and smart, Han Solo has a foul-mouthed, pragmatic wisdom that reminded me of the wisecracking *Star Wars* character who used irregular warfare strategies to fight the Empire. After I'd interviewed Han Solo about the basics of what the Army calls PSYOP, I still had a ton of questions. So he offered to give me a one-on-one PSYOP training session, or a condensed version of the classes he taught to Special Operations soldiers. I'm not sure he was prepared for me to take him up on it, but I jumped at the chance and he gamely went ahead with the plan. Over the next few weeks, he spent several hours on the phone with me, going over lesson plans and recent Army PSYOP textbooks that read like updated versions of Paul Linebarger's original manual on psychological warfare.

"There's a golden rule," Han Solo said as my instruction began. "We do not conduct PSYOP against US citizens. We cannot do that. That's a bright red line you cannot cross." And yet our own government had conducted psyops against us with a crappy Facebook quiz app. I wondered aloud why politicians would do things that the Army forbids in its official teaching material. "America loves to propagandize our own people but we [in PSYOP] are very cognizant of the power of social media," Han Solo replied. "We're apprehensive about second- and third-order effects." These "second- and third-order effects" could mean a message reaching the wrong audiences and causing a backlash. Or an operation could generate conspiracy theories that spiral wildly out of control, threatening lives. "[Social media] can be effective, but there are other ways to do it," Han Solo continued. "Junior soldiers who like TikTok and other stuff, they're more on board with it. Older folks like me and colonels—we've seen enough blowback on normal PSYOP like leaflets and billboards that we know it's best to tread lightly. Our adversaries don't give a fuck about blowback."

When he talked about "adversaries" like that, Russia came up a lot. That's partly because Russian operatives have meddled in recent US political debates online. But it was also because, as Han Solo put it, Russian psyops are all about "*maskirovka*, or baffling people with bullshit." Their government agencies flood social media with misinformation. As a second-order effect, it "confuses their own people too—nobody knows what's true, and they don't believe anything." Influence operations are so ubiquitous in Russia that everything seems to be fake news, and Han Solo believes "the domestic audience has become numb to it." They don't trust their government; they don't trust educators and scientists; and they don't trust one another.

Han Solo's worry, and that of many of his colleagues, is that right-wing operations like the ones masterminded by Cambridge Analytica have a similar effect on US citizens. Sociologist Jürgen

Habermas, a colleague of Theodor Adorno from the *Authoritarian Personality* group, called this a "legitimation crisis."[17] In such a crisis, social consensus and even simple communication become impossible because people disagree about the legitimacy of basic scientific and historical truths. When the US military engages in PSYOP, a legitimation crisis is the last thing they want. They're hoping to persuade people to take America's side in a conflict, which means they want to shift the adversary's political loyalties. If the target audience doesn't believe any institution or government can be legitimate, then there's no hope of that kind of persuasion. Russian operatives' strategy, by contrast, is to undermine persuasion with confusion.

During the Cold War, propaganda depended on the idea that most people had faith in one of the two Great Powers' belief systems: American democracy or Soviet communism. Doing PSYOP in the United States meant targeting communists and trying to sell them on US superiority. These days, as Han Solo explained during my instruction, we're still trying to sell our country's values and change our adversaries' actions—though obviously we're not targeting communists anymore. Now the targets range from Serbian nationalists in Bosnia during the 1990s to ISIS groups in Afghanistan during the early twenty-first century. But the goal is the same—to bring sympathizers over to our side and change their behavior—and the tactics are the same too. They're borrowed from advertising.

Han Solo walked me through a thick publication from the John F. Kennedy Special Warfare Center and School called simply *Military Information Support Operations (MISO) Process.*[18] The Army recently rebranded PSYOP as MISO, but many people, including

Han Solo, still use the term "PSYOP." Like Linebarger's book *Psychological Warfare*, the MISO textbook gives students instruction on how to craft a message, as well as how to target and disseminate it. Unlike Linebarger's book, it contains almost no philosophizing about the history of psychological warfare, and no speculation about how to launch a psychological disarmament campaign. Instead, it's full of detailed instructions on developing "products" (specific pieces of media, like a radio spot or a leaflet) and "series" (a psychological operation that contains many products). Examples come from modern conflicts in Iraq and Afghanistan. And there are worksheets—endless worksheets, full of checklists and boxes to fill in. Several chapters are devoted to proper procedures for going through the chain of command to get permission to launch a product. After almost seventy years of modern psychological operations in the Army, it should come as no surprise that a huge amount of bureaucratic cruft and new acronyms like MISO have developed around the process.

Some things do remain the same, though. PSYOP is still basically a weaponized advertising campaign. Operatives pick target audiences (TAs) and try to develop psychological profiles of them. PSYOP experts brainstorm ideas about the best way to reach their TAs, taking into account what kinds of media they like and who they look up to as sources of good information. A PSYOP specialist "has to be open-minded," Han Solo noted. To make a good product, he or she can't impose American ideas onto people who distrust Americans—an operative needs to be open to speaking the local language, and working within the cultures on the ground. The psywarrior has to understand what kinds of stories will evoke strong feelings in the audience she wants to reach, because cultural triggers vary widely from one nation to the next. Ajit Maan, author of the book *Narrative Warfare*[19] and a frequent consultant to the US military, told me that a psyop that works beautifully in the United States inevitably fails to hit its mark in China, and vice versa. That's why operatives in PSYOP units are instructed to identify trusted leaders and influencers within the TA, people who might be sympathetic to the United States and its allies and who are willing to help spread American messages to their community. Sometimes they conduct focus groups to workshop their messaging and make sure it aligns with local values. "It's easier to convince someone of a preexisting belief than to give them something brand-new and antithetical to their existing beliefs," Han Solo commented wryly.

"I'M GOING TO BE ANGRY FOR THE REST OF MY LIFE"

It all sounds pretty good in the classroom, but the reality is often grim. The US Army recommends that PSYOP students read a book called *Hearts and Mines: With the Marines in al Anbar; A Memoir of Psychological Warfare in Iraq*, by Russell Snyder, a soldier who served in a PSYOP battalion during the spring and summer of 2005. Snyder describes the difficulties PSYOP soldiers face in the field in spare, sometimes brutal terms. Every time he and his colleagues are deployed to an area, they face pushback because the Army isn't sure where they fit into a more traditional arsenal of weapons. The loudspeakers that Linebarger lauded in *Psychological Warfare* have become tools of torment rather than persuasion. When Snyder's unit rolls into a town across the river from suspected insurgents, he isn't supposed to persuade the enemy to surrender. Instead, they crank up their loudspeakers in the middle of the night, playing grossly amplified sounds of cats mating. They're hoping to be so annoying that the insurgents will start shooting and reveal their locations. When the ploy works, Snyder and his team hide from the ensuing firefight in an abandoned home with a lovely garden that he imagines must have taken years to cultivate. The situation is so morally gray that he gets no sense of triumph out of their PSYOP. Instead, he finds himself mourning for the innocent locals whose beautiful trees and flowers are being destroyed in the cross fire.

Even when he used leaflets instead of amplified cat screams, Snyder felt hopeless about the effectiveness of the message. At one point, he describes handing out "generic" leaflets about everything from proper sanitation to reporting insurgents to US authorities. Mostly, he writes, people took the leaflets with "a look of polite acknowledgement I usually reserve for those who pass out unsolicited religious pamphlets in front of local shopping centers."[20] Their leaflets were ignored. The only PSYOP product that seemed to work was humanitarian aid. "We used aid as a weapon to break the spirit of resistance and prove ourselves more capable than our enemy of providing life's necessities.... If we couldn't win their hearts by force of arms, we would buy them." But sadly, they never had enough money to pay for the damage that they had done to homes and infrastructure. Snyder offers a picture of PSYOP as an old-school blunt instrument in a world where enemy tactics are agile and conditions are rapidly changing.

Snyder's experience echoed what I heard from Han Solo as well as PSYOP experts like Mark Jacobson, who served as a foreign policy expert for the Department of Defense and as a reservist in Bosnia, Afghanistan, and many other regions. Jacobson told me the US military is falling behind the curve when it comes to psychological operations. He believes that the United States is perceived as not following through on the big promises made in its influence campaigns. A PSYOP product might persuade adversaries to put down their weapons, for example, by offering resources for defense, schools, food, and rebuilding a shattered infrastructure. But when the US government delivers inadequate aid, or none at all, American operatives and diplomats wind up sounding like liars. This creates a backlash within a population that feels betrayed, generating more sympathy for adversaries. Jacobson felt this sense of betrayal acutely in the wake of the Afghanistan withdrawal. "Now I understand why Vietnam vets, my mentors, were angry for the rest of their lives," he told me. "I'm going to be angry for the rest of my life."

Another problem is that the US military bureaucracy wasn't designed to deal with the speed and reach of social media. Adversaries post memes and videos online within hours or even minutes of major events, responding quickly to news and spinning it to their advantage. But as the MISO manual makes clear, a US PSYOP product has to be checked and rechecked as it slowly works its way up the chain of command before being approved. It might take months. This is a source of tremendous frustration for people in the military. On a 2021 episode of the Modern Warfare Institute's *Irregular Warfare Podcast*,[21] Raphael Cohen and Brent Colburn spoke grimly about how difficult it is to launch a PSYOP compared to a kinetic weapon. It takes only a few minutes to authorize a drone strike, but months to authorize a YouTube video intended to combat enemy memes and propaganda.

While the military's psychological campaigns founder, American politicians and right-wing operatives have gone online and modernized. Working with Cambridge Analytica's "mindfuck tool," Trump adviser Bannon and data scientist Wylie crafted a psychological campaign that targeted audiences on Facebook with a laser focus, guiding the Trump campaign's messaging. The 2016 Trump presidential campaign generated highly tailored ads on the platform, and their target audience was people who subconsciously craved authoritarian leadership. Trump's messaging often sounded like a mishmash of the emotional triggers that the *Authoritarian Personality* team warned against. Cynical appeals to power were rampant: Trump promised to make America "great" and strong. His team also pandered to various groups' ethnocentrism, painting refugees as nefarious invaders and calling Muslims terrorists.

The Trump campaign also targeted 3.5 million Black voters for what they called "deterrence," ads that were aimed at dissuading them from voting at all. Most of these ads showed a decontextualized clip of Hillary Clinton calling young kids in gangs "superpredators" in a 1996 speech, suggesting that she was hostile to Black people.[22] NAACP senior vice president Jamal Watkins told Britain's Channel 4 News that the deterrence ads were a digital version of voter suppression.[23] And they worked, too. Black voter turnout in 2016 declined by over 7 percentage points from the previous presidential election—the first decline in Black voter turnout in twenty years.[24]

But Cambridge Analytica wasn't responsible for all the microtargeted ads that drove and suppressed voter engagement in the 2016 election. They had a resourceful, chaotic ally. And this ally, as Han Solo would say, didn't give a fuck about blowback. In fact, that's exactly what they wanted.

WHEN AMERICANS TARGET AMERICANS

"America is used to being targeted by ads. We're exposed to ads and marketing from childhood, and that makes us easily played, easily messaged to," Han Solo told me. "Corporations spend trillions of dollars on ads because they work. It's the fastest way to get people to act on their beliefs. People are primed to be targeted." Mark Jacobson, the vice president of research at nonprofit organization Partnership for Public Service, spent his diplomatic career working on influence operations. He thinks Americans are vulnerable to propaganda "because we're so easily moved by advertising and the media. We let our hearts lead the way." Though marketing researchers find that it's often difficult to measure the effectiveness of online ads,[25] it's hard to argue with results like the ones we saw in the 2016 election.

Some of the most effective online manipulation of the American public came from a private Russian psyops firm called the Internet Research Agency (IRA). Once owned by Russian oligarch Yevgeny Prigozhin, head of private military company Wagner Group before his plane mysteriously exploded,[26] the IRA paid roughly $100,000 for targeted ad campaigns on Facebook and unleashed a new kind of psyop on the American people. The seeds for their campaign took root in early 2016, when the Russian intelligence organization GRU was trying a variety of methods to trick its way into the private email inboxes of Democratic National Committee members. As special counsel Robert S. Mueller's investigation subsequently revealed,[27] GRU hackers hit pay dirt when they gained access to a tranche of private emails from the Clinton campaign chairman, John Podesta. From there, the GRU gained access to other staffers' emails and documents, which they posted on a website called DCLeaks. But a giant blob of leaked emails and boring policy documents isn't worth anything unless someone carefully combs through them, identifies potentially scandalous bits, and turns those into stories that can be weaponized. That's where the IRA came into the picture.

In 2016, Facebook's chief information security officer, Alex Stamos, was alerted by an employee who specialized in Russian cyber warfare that they were seeing suspicious activity at the social media giant. GRU agents were accessing the accounts of people associated with Hillary Clinton's campaign, messaging Clinton staffers and journalists, snooping for any intel they could get. Stamos immediately reported it to the FBI, who confirmed his suspicion that it was coming from Russian state actors. That seemed to be the end of Facebook's troubles, until Stamos's team realized that there was another group of operatives from Russia who were messing with the social media platform in a very different way. Fake accounts and suspicious ads were popping up all over the place, full of disinformation and sensationalized reports about the DNC email leak. WikiLeaks got in on the action too, tweeting a link to the DCLeaks page.

But when Stamos tried to report the fake Facebook accounts and misinformation to the FBI, he recalled, "nobody in government had the responsibility or inclination to look for threat actors doing propaganda." They were worried about hacking, but "not trolling." Neither, he admitted, was Facebook. During the months when Stamos's team was frantically trying to deal with the mysterious DNC-leak-obsessed accounts, the IRA's messages were being amplified all across Facebook. People clicked on ads about the Democrats' secret emails, and shared them with friends. Eventually the mainstream media took notice. One story in particular got a lot of attention: emails from the leak suggested the DNC clearly favored Hillary Clinton's candidacy over Bernie Sanders's. This narrative was easy to spin up into a conspiracy theory that Sanders never had a chance because democracy was failing in the United States. As Han Solo taught me, this was a classic Russian strategy to create confusion. Instead of taking aim directly at the Clinton campaign, it undermined faith in the election itself. And that, as Bannon might say, was a great way to "disengage" voters. Why vote when the whole system is rigged to begin with?

The anti-Bernie conspiracy wasn't the only narrative to emerge from the social media storm unleashed by the IRA on Facebook. The leaked emails inspired the "#Pizzagate" conspiracy, a precursor to QAnon. People frequenting online community 4chan's right-wing forums identified "secret messages" in Podesta's emails. They believed they had uncovered an international conspiracy to kidnap children and rape them in the basement of Comet Ping Pong, a DC pizza joint popular with DNC workers. Late in 2016, a #Pizzagate believer drove to Comet Ping Pong with an AR-15 semiautomatic rifle. He threatened customers with it, searching the premises because he believed the Clinton campaign was raping children in the basement.[28] Ten months after the #Pizzagate attack, a shady figure named "QClearancePatriot" (later just Q) started posting in the /pol/ (Politically Incorrect) forums on 4chan, and the QAnon movement was born.[29] This bonkers sequence of events is a perfect example of the kind of chaos that IRA psyops unleash. The IRA didn't directly create QAnon. They simply inspired people to "do their own research" and uncover more conspiracies. Ordinary people using social media did the rest.

As conspiracy theories exploded online, Stamos and his team at Facebook were finishing a report about foreign information operations they were tracking—including the IRA's campaign. Stamos posted it on the company's newsfeed in April 2017, though Facebook leadership forced his team to remove all mentions of Russia.[30] The sanitized report has subsequently been removed from Facebook entirely, though it's easy to read a mirrored copy via the Internet Archive Wayback Machine.[31] In it, Stamos and his team described three elements of the IRA psyops methods: targeted data collection (stealing users' personal data, in this case from the DNC), false amplifiers (creating fake accounts to spread disinformation and sow distrust and confusion), and content creation (seeding false and real stories on Facebook, or to journalists, and other parties, sometimes via fake online personalities). They explained how it had all worked during the election:

> Malicious actors [leveraged] conventional and social media to share information stolen from other sources, such as email accounts, with the intent of harming the reputation of specific political targets. These incidents employed a relatively straightforward yet deliberate series of actions:
>
> - Private and/or proprietary information was accessed and stolen from systems and services [they're referring to the stolen DNC emails here];
> - Dedicated sites hosting this data were registered;
> - Fake personas were created on Facebook and elsewhere to point to and amplify awareness of this data;

- Social media accounts and pages were created to amplify news accounts of and direct people to the stolen data.
- From there, organic proliferation of the messaging and data through authentic peer groups and networks was inevitable.

Concurrently, a separate set of malicious actors engaged in false amplification using inauthentic Facebook accounts to push narratives and themes that reinforced or expanded on some of the topics exposed from stolen data.

Months after Stamos wrote this, Facebook finally allowed him and his colleagues to make a public statement linking the election meddling to Russia. Still, Stamos told me, he was frustrated that he couldn't reveal the full story, and he ultimately quit Facebook in 2018. "People [at Facebook] were pissed that we found [the IRA propaganda] and made a big deal about it, and created an obligation for the company to disclose."

The following year, Stamos helped to found the Stanford Internet Observatory, which is devoted to "the study of abuse in current information technologies." There, at last, he could openly share what had happened during his tenure at Facebook and continue researching it. His colleague at the Observatory, disinformation expert Renée DiResta, studied the IRA's amplification campaign and its relationship with the Russian government. She told the *Washington Post* that the IRA had done the heavy lifting when it came to media manipulation. Though the government hackers with the GRU were the ones who actually stole the DNC's emails, the agency was unable to get any social media pickup on them. "Maybe that's why the IRA exists," DiResta mused. "Maybe there's a recognition that this is a different form of propaganda."[32] In Russia, government hackers and corporate troll farms like the IRA have a hazy relationship, blurring the line between state-sponsored psyops and cultural influence campaigns. Inspired by the Russian model, private firms like Cambridge Analytica are offering their services to American politicians. But unlike the IRA, which targeted a foreign adversary, Cambridge Analytica was used by Americans against Americans.

BLACK OPS MARKETING CAMPAIGN

Since the US congressional investigations into the 2016 election, many analysts have shown that the IRA targeted ads at Americans in the same way Cambridge Analytica did. Simon Fraser University researchers Ahmed Al-Rawi and Anis Rahman, who teach in the School of Communication, analyzed 3,517 ads that the IRA paid for on Facebook and Instagram (owned by Facebook) between June 2015 and February 2017.[33] What the researchers discovered was that it took only a few thousand dollars to buy highly targeted ads—indistinguishable from legitimate advertising—that affected Americans' behavior in measurable ways. The IRA's ads led Facebook users to dozens of pages they had created for fake political and social groups, largely to foment racial divisions. The IRA focused on issues like gun control and police brutality as well as immigration. "These are sensitive topics they try to capitalize on, to mobilize the public and get their attention," Al-Rawi told me by video from his office in Vancouver, Canada. "They target specific online groups, and they try to make those messages appeal to these specific groups."

The goal of some IRA campaigns was to "activate" people, to get them off Facebook and doing something in the real world. In one case, the IRA set up two opposing Facebook groups in Texas—both fake—called Heart of Texas and United Muslims of America.[34] In May 2016, when they had amassed enough followers, the IRA's Heart of Texas announced on their page a "Stop Islamification of Texas" protest in front of the Islamic Da'wah Center of Houston. Then the IRA announced a counterprotest against "Save Islamic Knowledge" on the United Muslims of America page for the same day. Unwitting followers showed up to fight it out in real life, never knowing that they were all victims of Russian psyops.

Other ads were intended to alienate Black voters from US politics. Al-Rawi and Rahman discovered that over a hundred ads were specifically targeted at Black people in Ferguson, St. Louis County, Missouri, and Baltimore, Maryland, after the police shooting of Michael Brown, the death of Freddie Gray, and subsequent Black Lives Matter uprisings. They also targeted Detroit and Washington, DC, which have large Black communities. Many of these ads emphasized police brutality and violence against Black people, suggesting that neither Democrats nor Republicans would fix the problem. Rather than pushing Black voters off Facebook and into action, these ads offered a nihilistic view that nothing would ever change. Given that Cambridge Analytica also had a project to suppress Black votes, it's clear that there were multiple sources of propaganda aimed at persuading Black people to stay home on Election Day.

The IRA also amplified some of the Trump campaign's messages by targeting anyone in a southern-border state who was anxious about immigration. Al-Rawi said he's seen a lot of hateful propaganda in his professional career, but the IRA's campaign was one of the most extreme. "They were always trying to push the limits," he said. "There were a few ads discussing immigrants that were so racist that they equated Mexican immigrants with cockroaches." He pointed out that this was the same rhetoric Nazis used against Jews during the Holocaust. "The way they represented refugees and immigrants is horrific," he added. "I don't even see it on far-right sites. They pushed the limits for a reason—they want to desensitize people toward these issues to make it OK to talk about refugees in this way."

Al-Rawi said that he's started describing groups like the IRA operatives as "disguised elites." That's because their modus operandi is to disguise themselves as concerned citizens trying to organize in their local communities, but in fact, they are actually elite operatives with a significant advertising budget, state approval, and hundreds of dedicated agents who spend their days posting propaganda and garbage memes. To win, all a group like the IRA has to do is create a wrathful mix of brain fog online—and, they hope, offline too.

The story of the 2016 election feels like ancient history now, partly because there have been so many developments in social media psyops since then. QAnon has evolved into a major political force, with adherents like Georgia Republican congressional representative Marjorie Taylor Greene. During the 2020 election, President Trump spread misinformation about the election, suggesting that leftists were tampering with voting machines and mail-in ballots during the pandemic, lending credibility to conspiracy theories that seemed marginal back in 2016. Facebook shut down as many of the Russian-operated accounts as possible, and made some effort to label misinformation on the platform, but it was too late. Right-wing activists online took up where the IRA left off, using many of the same authoritarian messages.

In the lead-up to the 2020 presidential election, an anonymous Facebook executive told *Politico* that "right-wing populism is always more engaging" because it arouses "an incredibly strong, primitive emotion" with appeals to "nation, protection, the other, anger, fear." The executive shrugged off Facebook's responsibility for the spread of authoritarian-flavored content by saying that it wasn't "invented by social media" because it "was there in the [19]30s."[35] In other words, Facebook didn't invent fascism; it started with Nazism in the 1930s, and Facebook can't help if users want to amplify it. But ex-Facebooker Adam Conner, now with the Center for American Progress, disagreed. "Facebook is not a mirror—the newsfeed algorithm is an accelerant," he told *Politico*. Facebook continued to boost far-right propaganda, with violent results. Inspired by Trump's false claims of a stolen election, a mob of right-wing insurrectionists rioted in the US Capitol on January 6, 2021, attempting to overturn Joe Biden's win. Some threatened to kill Democratic members of Congress and Vice President Mike Pence. Instead of coming up with a robust, transparent system for dealing with psyops from abroad and at home, Facebook rebranded as Meta and briefly tried to create a virtual reality "metaverse" platform. When that failed, Meta launched Twitter clone Threads, which is as vulnerable to trolls and operatives as Facebook is. In 2023, the company determined that politician Robert F. Kennedy Jr. would be permitted to spread misinformation about vaccines across its platforms, including Instagram.[36] Lying is permitted, even when it endangers public health.

That said, the clickability of right-wing populism on social media is not isolated to Facebook. Twitter (now known as X) has become a radical-right stronghold in the wake of Elon Musk's purchase of it in 2022. IRA-style chaos propaganda will likely be amplified to new audiences as people flee X and sign up for new, less centrally regulated platforms like Mastodon and Bluesky, as well as the Meta-owned Threads. A 2023 lawsuit in Missouri about political jawboning aimed to stop the Biden administration from asking social media companies to block material that was false or misleading. The case was just one part of a larger right-wing movement to prevent governments and civic organizations from working with social media to stop misinformation about elections, public health, and more. Cumulatively, this movement has had a chilling effect.[37] YouTube, owned by Google, is no longer taking down videos that claim the 2020 election was stolen.[38] Meta, Facebook's parent company, is no longer blocking COVID misinformation,[39] and in 2023 the company laid off members of a global team that countered election disinformation and harassment.[40]

All these developments have led to a public sphere where American political organizations can target Americans with psyops. Cambridge Analytica may be gone, but most of the owners and directors from Cambridge Analytica's parent company SCL have now formed a political consulting company, Emerdata Limited, which is financed by the Mercers.[41] Of all the major players in the 2016 election psywar, only whistleblower Christopher Wylie has stepped away from political manipulation: in 2019, he joined fashion company H&M and has turned his powers of data analysis back to marketing clothes. In a 2022 interview on Telegram, Yevgeny Prigozhin, the late Russian oligarch who owned the IRA, talked about his company's role in US elections: "Gentlemen, we interfered, we interfere and we will interfere . . . carefully, precisely, surgically. . . . During our pinpoint operations, we will remove both kidneys and the liver at once."[42]

IT'S JUST A JOKE, MAN

Methods of information warfare that seemed novel in 2016 are now a part of our everyday lives. We have officially entered an age of what experts call "stochastic terrorism," a term that has become increasingly popular in the last decade to explain random violence inspired by online media. The gunman who showed up at Comet Ping Pong with an AR-15, inspired by #Pizzagate, is a stochastic terrorist, as are members of the January 6 mob at the US Capitol and many mass shooters, like white supremacist Dylann Roof, who murdered nine people at Bible study in a Black church. Like those latent fascists whom Else Frenkel-Brunswik and her colleagues studied in *The Authoritarian Personality*, a stochastic terrorist is someone who becomes activated and violent when triggered by outside pressures. Today, that pressure comes from social media and other kinds of propaganda that demonize marginalized groups like Black people, Jews, immigrants, and the LGBT community. Mass shootings in synagogues, Black churches, mosques, Asian-owned businesses, and gay community spaces remind us that culture war, like psywar, is always on the brink of erupting into violence.

Juliette Kayyem, former assistant secretary at the Department of Homeland Security, describes stochastic terrorism as "a pattern that can't be predicted precisely but can be analyzed statistically." Put simply, we can predict that terrorism will happen, just not where or when. What makes this kind of terrorism "stochastic," or chaotic, is that no one can be sure which triggered individuals will become violent. And it's hard to pin down who is inciting the violence, because, as Kayyem puts it, "the language [of the propaganda] is vague enough that it leaves room for plausible deniability."[43] Often, the rhetoric of stochastic terrorism is masked as "just a joke" or "just trolling." It's worth noting that the "just a joke" defense goes back to the early days of Nazism. Sociologist Leo Löwenthal, a colleague of the *Authoritarian Personality* team, wrote a book in the wake of World War II called *Prophets of Deceit*, where he chronicled how pundits advocating for Hitler's genocidal policies would claim slyly they were merely doing comedy.[44] It's hard to know who our enemies are when Americans borrow our adversaries' strategies and treat one another like enemy combatants.

Organizations like the IRA and Cambridge Analytica, working with governments and activated citizens, have created a media environment where it's difficult to know what's true and which institutions are legitimate. It's a situation that Paul Linebarger described back in the 1940s, when he was researching how Nazi Germany and the Soviet Union affected people's minds, making them "propaganda-dizzy." Bombarded by disinformation, he wrote, a "propaganda-dizzy man . . . sees in everything its propaganda content and nothing else. . . . Nothing is innocent; nothing is pleasurable; everything is connected with his diseased apprehension of power."[45] Here Linebarger might easily be describing #Pizzagate and QAnon acolytes, who find liberal and "woke" conspiracies woven into everything. Every political speech is a potential secret message. And every online troll is a potential mass shooter.

Even storytelling itself has become a source of deadly conflict. Right-wing social media mobs turn media franchises like Star Wars and Lord of the Rings into opportunities to attack anyone who disagrees with conservative takes on race, gender, and morality. Ben Collins, who covers extremism for NBC, noted that American right-wing movements learned their lessons from psyops experts well: "The American Far Right . . . [is] very good at storytelling," he told *On the Media*. "It's worldbuilding, that's what it is, really."[46] Worldbuilding is what Linebarger and other science fiction authors brought to psyops, and now the weapons they designed for use in total war are being deployed in cultural battles among Americans.

Psychological warfare in the time of stochastic terrorism has morphed into culture war—the battleground shrouds America in its fog, regardless of whether we are formal combatants. But we can find a pathway through the smoke by remembering the history of American psychological war, born during the Indian Wars and codified in the Cold War. We know what kinds of weapons are stashed in America's psychological ordnance depot. If an operative is using lies to persuade, if they threaten violence, if they treat their fellow citizens like foreign adversaries—then they are armed with military-grade psychological weapons. In our current social media psywars, we can witness in real time as weapons once used in military conflicts are deployed in domestic culture wars. The results are as destructive and traumatic as wartime propaganda.

Still, there is something important that we can learn from the history of psyops. As Ghost Dancers proved during the Indian Wars, there is always a resistance.

PART II

CULTURE WARS

CHAPTER 4

BAD BRAINS

Though the line between psychological war and culture war can be blurry in the United States, there is one way to tell the difference. In a culture war, the combatants are all Americans, fighting over domestic issues. Still, culture warriors often question whether certain groups of people are "truly" Americans. The reasons for this are complicated, but one obvious historical precedent comes from the original US Constitution, which defined several types of people living in the country as partial or non-citizens. Enslaved Black individuals were mere fractions of people (three-fifths, to be exact); Indigenous people were described as not taxable because they were not American citizens; women, who could neither vote nor own property, were not mentioned at all. Over the next two centuries, many of the nation's bloodiest culture wars were fought over who gets to claim American personhood. These battles led to some key constitutional amendments, such as the ones granting suffrage to freed slaves and women, as well as laws allowing Indigenous tribes and immigrants more freedoms. But the culture wars over who counts as an American, or even as a human being, are far from over. They return, like repressed memories, to retraumatize us.

In a culture war, combatants justify using psyops against people living in the United States by framing specific groups as a foreign power, an "other" whose influence has become dangerous to the nation. Often, these groups are similar to ones defined as outsiders in the Constitution: people who came from other countries, by choice or in chains; Indigenous nations; and groups omitted from the Constitution, like women and LGBT people.

Psyops in a culture war take a different form from those in a kinetic war. PSYOP specialists in the military have a singular goal: convince the enemy to change their behavior. Culture warriors have two goals: convince Americans that some of their fellow citizens are the enemy; and convince "the enemy" that there is something deeply wrong with their minds, and therefore they are not qualified to demand greater freedoms and personal dignity. A culture-war attack divides the nation into two groups: those with good brains and those with bad ones.

Nowhere is this more obvious than in political debates and pseudo-scientific questions about the brains of Black people. There is a long history behind this conflict, which has broken out again in recent years. Ever since the first enslaved Africans were brought to the Americas in the seventeenth century, white Americans have debated whether to educate Black people. Many slave owners refused to teach enslaved Africans to read and write; their subsequent illiteracy was used to justify the idea that Black people were not smart enough to read. This is why many escaped slaves, including Frederick Douglass, described learning to read as a crucial step toward freedom.[1]

With the abolition of slavery and the passage of the Fourteenth Amendment, Black men established their intellectual credibility by voting and, in a few cases, holding elected office. Still, the battle raged on. Joining the fray in the late nineteenth century was anthropologist Francis Galton, who popularized the idea of eugenics in his 1869 book, *Hereditary Genius*. He believed intelligence was an inherited trait, and suggested that Black, Brown, and poor people's brains were biologically inferior to those of upper-class whites. Many American scientists welcomed Galton's ideas. Indeed, Harvard University zoologist Louis Agassiz had been arguing since the 1840s that Black people were a separate species from whites.[2]

It was in this cultural environment that the psyops known as Jim Crow laws took aim at Black Americans, forcing them to use separate facilities from whites during the late nineteenth and twentieth centuries. Segregation made the Black community appear to be a kind of foreign adversary that white people needed to keep at bay. Very quickly, the Black community began organizing defenses against this attack. Historically Black colleges and universities (HBCUs) functioned in part as a potent counter-psyop under Jim Crow. Internationally lauded Black artists and intellectuals of the early 1900s Harlem Renaissance, as well as high-profile Black scientists and public servants, offered models of Black excellence. Still, white people continued to debate whether Black people truly were the mental equals of whites. The culture war over the Black mind is why the 1954 Supreme Court ruling in *Brown v. Board of Education* was such a huge win for the civil rights movement. In a unanimous decision, the court found that segregated education was unconstitutional and Black children deserved the same schooling as white ones. In a sense, the federal government had finally declared that Black and white minds were equal.

But laws and history have never stopped culture warriors from recycling old psyops as if they were brand-new. Debates over Black intelligence reignited in the mid-1990s as part of a conservative push to end all affirmative action programs, including in higher education. During the '90s "bell curve wars," as they came to be called,[3] social scientists suggested that Black people as a group were genetically incapable of achieving the same levels of intelligence that whites and other races could. This weaponized rhetorical strategy undermined Black people's status in the eyes of their fellow Americans, while taking aim at Black people's views of their own mental capabilities. As we'll see, the '90s version of this culture war was also fueled by a science fiction story about how stupidity would destroy America.

EUGENICS REBOOTED

In 1994, Charles Murray was starting a promotional tour for what became one of the most widely discussed books of the 1990s: *The Bell Curve: Intelligence and Class Structure in American Life.* His co-author, Richard Herrnstein, had recently died, and that meant Murray had to promote the book on his own. The hype around its publication was unusually intense, especially for an 845-page social science book packed with charts and graphs. Murray's publicity team would not release preview copies to reviewers, because the author worried that his book would be "wrongly construed" without proper context.[4] His team hand-picked a few reporters to write about his work, among them the *New York Times* journalist Jason DeParle. He shadowed Murray in the days before *The Bell Curve* book launch, flying on Rupert Murdoch's private plane with him to Aspen, Colorado, where the social scientist would be feted at a mansion owned by one of his many fans. It sounded like the life of a celebrity.

Murray was living the high life of a right-wing culture hero—beloved by Ronald Reagan and lionized by a generation of conservatives who defined themselves in opposition to the 1960s civil rights movement. He became their favorite public intellectual by writing manifestos about why the wealthy owed nothing to the poor. In the 1980s, Murray had published a hugely popular book called *Losing Ground*, where he argued that welfare programs caused crime, worsened poverty in Black communities, and encouraged women to become single mothers. Murray deployed a lot of infographics and footnotes to explain why his perspective was validated by science, and rationality became his brand. His messaging worked so well because he smuggled an emotional appeal to racial and class bias inside a seemingly evidence-based analysis.

As he flew to Colorado, Murray pulled out a laptop to show DeParle some data that fueled his analysis in *The Bell Curve*. There was a spreadsheet full of personal statistics on over twelve thousand Americans—including IQ, race, salary, educational level, age, marital status, and more—taken from the National Longitudinal Survey of Youth (NLSY), a multigenerational study conducted by the US Bureau of Labor Statistics and widely used for social science research. Because of his academic credentials, Murray had also gotten some NLSY data that isn't released to the general public, including where participants lived and went to school.[5] He and Herrnstein had crunched the data to measure relationships between IQ and financial success. Entering a formula into the spreadsheet on his laptop, Murray tallied the average difference in salary between a person with 100 IQ and a person with 115: $6,654 a year. For every 15 points of IQ, he noted with satisfaction, a person got a significant boost in income.

He was talking about the idea at the heart of *The Bell Curve*, which is that intelligence is what determines people's economic fate. And here's the kicker: according to Murray and Herrnstein, Black people were statistically more likely to fall on the low end of the IQ spectrum, as were unwed mothers and the poor generally. That meant the "bell" in the book's eponymous probability-distribution graph was occupied by middle-class, married white people[6] with average IQs. Their takeaway? Black people had less wealth in the United States because of intellectual failings. Certain groups were simply too "dull" to succeed in the modern US economy, no matter how much help the government gave them. Welfare and affirmative action would destroy America, Murray and Herrnstein claimed, because such programs made it easier for the "dull" to survive. The authors concluded with what they considered a terrifying scenario. Poor people were breeding in enormous numbers, they wrote, thanks to unwed mothers. Soon, *The Bell Curve* warned, the nation would be dragged down by a "dysgenic trend" of increasingly unintelligent people.

Though the book was roundly criticized by experts, receiving a sharp rejoinder from the American Psychological Association[7] and countless debunkings from political scientists,[8] it nevertheless resonated with Americans. *The Bell Curve* sold two hundred thousand copies in its first month of publication.[9] Charles Murray made the rounds on national TV and radio programs to discuss his ideas. Debates over the book were so feverish that even President Bill Clinton weighed in to say that he disagreed with its premise about Black IQs,[10] though he would eventually sign a welfare-reform bill that was influenced by Murray's research. *The Bell Curve* was a gift to conservative policymakers, who used it to attack affirmative action programs. Pat Buchanan, a conservative adviser to Reagan who championed the idea of "culture war" in a 1992 speech, had been arguing against affirmative action programs since the 1970s by citing Herrnstein's early research.[11] Tech billionaire Peter Thiel, who became one of Trump's main allies in Silicon Valley, mentioned *The Bell Curve* in a 1996 commentary on why affirmative action had failed.[12] Armed with Herrnstein and Murray's research, these powerful men helped persuade Americans to gut affirmative action. In 1996, Californians voted to end affirmative action programs in governmental institutions including higher education, and Texas followed suit;[13] in 2023, a Supreme Court ruling banned these programs nationwide. Even three decades after its publication, *The Bell Curve* is the subject of wrathful op-eds in venues from *Scientific American*[14] to YouTube.[15]

We can see many signs that this salvo in the culture wars benefited from techniques used for psychological war. First, *The Bell Curve* cast Black people as second-class "others" by proposing a Jim Crow law of intelligence. According to the experts, Murray and Herrnstein suggested, Black people's struggles were caused not by systemic racism but instead by their defective minds. What made this message so effective was the authors' appeal to science and facts. Readers couldn't go more than a few pages without finding a handy chart, such as one titled "The High-IQ Occupations Are Also the Well-Paid Occupations."[16] It sounded rational. White people who would never join the KKK or openly espouse white supremacist views felt comfortable sharing this seemingly scholarly book with friends. Murray had been honing this form of respectable racist rhetoric for over a decade. As he said in regard to *Losing Ground*, his previous book: "A huge number of well-meaning whites fear that they are closet racists, and this book tells them they are not. It's going to make them feel better about things they already think but do not know how to say."[17] *The Bell Curve*'s data about higher IQs being correlated with higher wages gave them a way to say it.

But, as scientists are fond of saying, correlation does not equal causation. *The Bell Curve* provided absolutely no evidence that high IQ *causes* wealth. This supposedly scientific book was a weapon, deploying the half-truths and outright fabulations of a psyop to argue that Black people and the poor were America's true enemies.

THE SEDUCTIONS OF FALSE RATIONALITY

There are two basic falsehoods at the heart of Herrnstein and Murray's book: one is that there is a widely agreed-upon system for measuring intelligence accurately, and the other is that welfare will lead to a dark future that sounds a lot like the 2006 movie *Idiocracy*, where Americans have become dim-witted slackers led by a Black president.[18] To persuade their readers, Murray and Herrnstein swaddled these lies in false rationality, making their opinions look like facts.

The Bell Curve's premise depends on the existence of a reliable way to measure intelligence, but there is no such thing. Most social scientists take a dim view of IQ scores as a predictor of wealth and success, and the test has been controversial since its inception in the early 1900s.[19] IQ testing was popularized in the United States by Stanford professor Lewis Terman, a eugenicist who wrote in 1916 that intelligence tests would be used in the future to identify "defectives" and put them "under the surveillance and protection of society." Terman added enthusiastically that this would "ultimately result in curtailing the reproduction of feeble-mindedness and in the elimination of . . . crime, pauperism, and industrial inefficiency."[20] IQ tests were, in other words, designed to single out and eliminate groups of people whom eugenicists deemed "defective." And in case it wasn't obvious who that might be, Terman wrote that Black people possessed a "dullness [that] seems to be racial."

At that time, a major opponent of IQ testing was Horace Mann Bond, a social scientist who taught at several historically Black universities and became the first Black president of Lincoln University in Pennsylvania. In 1924, he warned that IQ tests were "insidious propaganda which . . . seeks to demonstrate that the Negro is intellectually and physically incapable of assuming the dignities, rights and duties which devolve upon him as a member of modern society."[21] He urged Black intellectuals to become "active agent[s]" in the fight against IQ testing. Bond's clarion call was taken up by several Black educators of his generation. In the 1930s, Howard Hale Long decided to conduct his own intelligence tests with Black children. A Harvard-trained psychologist who was superintendent of the Washington, DC, public school system from 1925 to 1948, Long was in the perfect position to do this kind of work. He tested Black children from a variety of backgrounds and found that their test scores had nothing to do with "innate" intelligence—instead, these scores were correlated with socioeconomic status, location, and educational opportunities.[22]

While Bond and Long focused on debunking the IQ tests with research, sympathetic members of the media chimed in with their own tart criticisms. Walter Lippmann, author of *Public Opinion*, published a series of anti-IQ articles in the *New Republic* in 1922, calling intelligence testing a "fad" comparable to "palmistry."[23] Pushback against IQ as a measure of intelligence has a history as long as IQ testing itself.

Needless to say, Herrnstein and Murray ignored decades of research on IQ. Even if they hadn't, it wouldn't have mattered. Despite constantly referring to IQ, the authors didn't actually have IQ scores for any of the people in the dataset they used. Intrepid readers who made it to the end of the book would discover this in appendix 2, "Technical Issues Regarding the National Longitudinal Survey of Youth." There, Murray and Herrnstein revealed that they were using intelligence scores from the Armed Services Vocational Aptitude Battery, part of the Armed Forces Qualification Test, designed by the military to measure the "cognitive ability" of potential soldiers in their late teens.[24] This score isn't the same as an IQ score, and Herrnstein and Murray admitted that many of the people in the NLSY took the test when they were younger than the intended subjects. Then, in appendix 3, Murray and Herrnstein confessed that scores on the Armed Services Vocational Aptitude Battery were actually a measure of the subject's educational background and not of raw, biological intelligence. After acknowledging that their intelligence data was deeply flawed, they carried on using it to buttress their argument. Like a classic psyops product, *The Bell Curve* was intentionally misleading. It was designed to persuade Americans that eugenics was actually a pretty rational idea.

Murray and Herrnstein pulled a lot of their scientific evidence from studies published in *Mankind Quarterly*, a journal founded in 1960 by a group of segregationists and bankrolled by the Pioneer Fund, a group known for funding proponents of eugenics.[25] Perhaps not surprisingly, *The Bell Curve* begins with a celebration of the work of Francis Galton, who popularized eugenics in the 1860s. The authors framed themselves as valiantly continuing the work Galton had begun 126 years before to prove that white people are smarter than other races. But this wasn't just an argument about white supremacy. It was about whiteness under threat. Like their eugenicist muse, they feared that Black and Brown people, as well as "dull" immigrants, were causing a dysgenic trend that had to be stopped.

Angela Saini, author of a history of eugenics called *Superior: The Return of Race Science*, said that most people associate eugenics with Nazism during World War II, but it showed up in countless other conflicts. "It was one of the underlying philosophies of colonialism," she explained. It rationalized the American slave system as well as "American exceptionalism, this idea that the colonists who went to America from Europe were destined to be there, and they were chosen to rule." But after the Holocaust, race science became a marginal, shunned discipline. In the 1960s and '70s, people like Herrnstein and Murray would have been "complete outsiders," Saini explained. The eugenicists who founded *Mankind Quarterly* "were criticized for the controversial things they said." Herrnstein and Murray successfully revived race science with *The Bell Curve*. Since then, ideas borrowed from eugenics have gradually become acceptable again, especially among pundits. Former

Fox News commentator Tucker Carlson evoked it in monologues about "the great replacement," an age-old conspiracy theory that suggests Jews are trying to replace white Americans with people of color and immigrants.[26] "Now there's a problem because the internet has allowed these people to amass followers online in quite large numbers," Saini mused. "You can hear that kind of rhetoric among politicians now, these subtly eugenic ideas. . . . They love this kind of pseudoscience because it gives them [a] feeling of intellectual credibility."[27]

This "feeling of intellectual credibility" is also a formidable weapon to use against anyone who disagrees. On the internet, this weapon is often called tone policing. Eugenicists accuse critics of being emotional and irrational, especially if those critics come from one of the groups deemed inferior. *The Bell Curve* adds additional artillery to this psyop, since the entire point of the book is that Black and Brown people are "dull." The not-so-hidden insinuation is that your average Black person will be incapable of appreciating the scientific discoveries of white people like Murray and Herrnstein. Black opposition to eugenics is portrayed as angry and out of control, a symptom of Black inferiority. False rationality often succeeds as an influence strategy because of this built-in defense against criticism. Anyone who disagrees is deemed too irrational or too stupid to understand the "truth" that Herrnstein and Murray pulled out of their spreadsheets of data.

RACIST FUTURISM

Murray gleefully told DeParle that his data was "social science pornography."[28] He wasn't wrong. Like most pornography, *The Bell*

Curve was long on feels and short on facts. And there was one particular fact that Murray and Herrnstein couldn't handwave away. When they compared Black and white people with similar intelligence scores, the substantial difference in economic outcomes between the two groups shrank by 77 percent. Smart Black people escaped poverty almost as often as smart white ones, they found, and yet whites still came out ahead. To explain this glaring discrepancy, Murray and Herrnstein turned to full-blown storytelling without even the pretense of evidence-based analysis.

First they invented a statistical category that they called the Middle Class Values Index, or MCV.[29] It measured a "set of behaviors" that they associated with "solid citizens."[30] There was no bell curve for MCV—either you had MCV or you didn't, and different values were measured for men and women. A man scored a "yes" on the MCV if he had a high school diploma, was employed for at least a year, had never been in jail, and was still married to his first wife. Women scored a "yes" if they had a high school diploma, never had a child out of wedlock, had never been in jail, and were still married to their first husbands. Murray and Herrnstein argued that "ethnic differences"[31] in MCV scores explained why Black and Brown people did not succeed even if they had high IQs. (Amusingly, Murray himself had a low MCV score: he was married to his second wife at the time *The Bell Curve* came out, and his childhood friend described their run-in with police as teenagers when they lit a cross on fire.)[32] When they couldn't prove that Black people had bad brains, Murray and Herrnstein came up with a test to prove that they had bad souls. Black people weren't joining the middle class, they argued, because they lacked the right ineffable values to become "solid citizens."

After touting the results of their absurd "middle-class values" test, the authors launched into what they admitted was sheer speculation.[33] In a chapter called "The Way We Are Headed," they spun up a near-future scenario, much like a science fiction story, where eugenics turns out to be reality. Rich and poor evolve into separate species. Soon the world is ruled by a small "cognitive elite" who take over the biggest corporations, local and federal governments, universities, and the media. They amass a tremendous amount of wealth and bend the nation to their will, but this smart minority is isolated from the reality that lurks outside their fancy corporate boardrooms. Crowding the "slums" around them is a rapidly expanding underclass whose cognitive abilities are decreasing with each generation. This is where the story starts to sound a lot like the movie *Idiocracy*, about a man who awakens from a hibernation experiment to find himself stranded in a dumbed-down future America. In *The Bell Curve*, "low intelligence" people can't compete for jobs with their cognitive superiors. Instead of working, they languish in prisons, do drugs, and have children out of wedlock. Though they were describing the future of poor people generally, Murray and Herrnstein make sure to let readers know that this future would begin with Black millennials: "A large majority of the next generation of blacks in the inner city is growing up without fathers and with limited cognitive ability."

Then the story takes an even darker turn. A repressive "custodial state" builds "a high-tech and more lavish version of the Indian reservation" for the mindless underclass.[34] Soon, poor people are no longer entrusted with money, because they can't figure out how to spend it. So the custodial state buys them everything they need, and raises their children for them. After all, unwed mothers are mentally unfit to care for children. As each generation becomes duller, poor people cease to understand why marriage is a good idea, and don't have the intellectual capacity to hold their marriages together. Cognitive elites pour even more money into the custodial state, hoping that more social spending will change the dysgenic fate of the poor. They fund the creation of specialized surveillance technology to track poor people, who are apparently wandering around in a daze. Criminals are given "neighborhood arrest," as the inner cities go from being reservations to free-range prisons. The more money the elites shower on these "irresponsible" and "welfare-dependent" people, the worse things get. Finally, "a significant part of the population must be made permanent wards of the state." As Michael Stern wrote in a review for the *San Francisco Chronicle*, "It's a pseudoscholarly dystopia, a nonfiction *Brave New World* misrepresented by its authors and their allies as disinterested scholarship."[35]

It's also a completely made-up story with a goal my PSYOP instructor Han Solo drummed into my head: it is intended to change Americans' behavior. *The Bell Curve* concluded with a series of policy recommendations based on preventing the authors' fantasy future. Policymakers, they wrote, should divert social spending to youngsters who are members of "cognitive elites." Welfare and affirmative action programs should be eliminated, since they will only create a "custodial state" that encourages poor people to breed. Immigration policies should favor "smarter" groups from the global North. And the poor should be penalized for having children out of wedlock. The underclass would require strict moral guidelines to keep its members in check, the authors postulated, because their low intelligence prevents them from choosing the right set of values. "Inequality of endowments, including intelligence, is a reality," they concluded. "It is time for America once again to try living with inequality."[36] Better to let the poor suffer and die than survive and breed more like themselves.

"WHITE SUPREMACY IS A PSYOP"

UC Berkeley English professor emeritus Ishmael Reed, an Afrofuturist author and critic, told me what it was like in the mid-1990s when people discussed *The Bell Curve* as if it were some kind of scientific breakthrough. He felt like the only reasonable response was laughter. After all, how could you take the custodial-state dystopia scenario seriously? Reed had honed his absurdist sense of humor in his 1972 novel, *Mumbo Jumbo*, which is about an alternate 1920s America where a secret society with ties to the Knights Templar tries to stop Black artists from spreading a jazz mind virus that makes people want to dance. Reed liked to satirize racism; it was a counter-psyop, a way of showing how utterly ridiculous it was to treat Black culture like a disease—or, in today's political terms, a "woke mind virus." He also reminded his readers that pundits like Herrnstein and Murray were part of a whole industry devoted to swaying public opinion for money. In 1995, he snarked about *The Bell Curve* in the *Washington Post*, writing that "racism is . . . one of the fastest growth industries in this country." He joked that it "would solve the unemployment problem in Oakland if they would funnel their profits back."[37]

When he was young, Reed told me, education felt to him like a psyop because nobody talked about race—or at least, no race other than the white one. "People of color . . . had to find out about our traditions from the streets," he recalled. Universities offered only the kind of false rationality peddled by *The Bell Curve*, a "curriculum that glorifies things that never happened." When I asked what he thought about *The Bell Curve*'s influence today, he joked that it's still about "selling racism." Current debates over cancel culture seemed to him just a continuation of the same rhetoric about Black people ruining America. Once again, white people were discussing what to do with Black people, and Black people's opinions were drowned out. "You look at these people talking about cancel culture, like Bill Maher and David Brooks—they reach more people in one week than all the ethnic studies courses in the last twenty years," he said. He described the situation as an asymmetric culture war, where Black critics like himself could occasionally land a great zinger in a national newspaper but rarely had the reach of a television pundit.

The Bell Curve proposes what is essentially a Jim Crow law of the mind, and there is a long history of Black resistance to it. This psyop was most effective against white people, changing their minds about how to deal with poverty and systemic inequality. While many white people bought into the book's lies, Black people fought back. Even though the IQ psyop was aimed at undermining Black people's confidence in their intellectual abilities, it wasn't effective.

This is a classic failure mode in psyops: the propagandist's own biases cause him to underestimate or simply miss his target. Edward Hunter, the journalist and maybe-operative who wrote *Brainwashing: The Story of Men Who Defied It*, described a similar phenomenon during the Cold War. As we saw in chapter 1, some of Hunter's claims were pretty much unsubstantiated propaganda about evil Chinese "brainwash" factories. But there is one section of the book that stands out as a rare moment of evidence-based journalism. Hunter made a point of seeking out Black men who had been POWs during the Korean War, and presented their narratives as evidence that Black soldiers have a far greater capacity to resist brainwashing than white ones. He ascribed it partly to the hardships that many Black men had already endured in a racist society, forcing them to lead humble lives without much comfort: "Fellows who had had a comfortable life, never deprived of anything [were easily broken]. Men who had lived simple, down-to-earth lives, who weren't afraid of going without comforts because they had done it often before, couldn't be cracked so easily."[38]

The men Hunter interviewed said that even in the POW camps, the Black prisoners had a strong sense of community and selfhood that their captors didn't seem to understand. Corporal Robert Stell, the first US POW to be released in a prisoner exchange in 1953, told Hunter that

> [the communists] . . . felt the Negro was craving for something the white man had, that he wanted to copy the whites. They didn't realize that during all of his past hardships, the Negro had developed something of his own, distinctly his. If the Chinese communists had taken the Negroes seriously, they would have realized that the Negro put his own taste into everything he got from the white man. They would have known that the Negro had his own characteristics and a character of his own.[39]

Essentially, Stell argued that the communists made the same mistake as their American adversaries: they thought of them as second-class, without any culture of their own. They understood nothing about Black history and tastes, and crafted psyops that broke down white people. But the Black prisoners supported one another, praying, singing, and sneaking a little bit of cannabis into the prison to ease their pain. They could resist their captors' attempts at psychological torture because they had already learned to dodge white supremacist propaganda at home. Far from being mentally inferior, these were men with more developed critical faculties than their white counterparts.

Unfortunately, seeing through a psyop doesn't make it disappear—especially when the warriors who produced it have the bully pulpit of the media and serve in Congress. *The Bell Curve*'s influence has continued to grow in the twenty-first century. Charles Murray published a sequel to *The Bell Curve* in 2020 called *Human Diversity: The Biology of Gender, Race, and Class*. He's inspired a new generation of "race realists" and "human biodiversity" researchers, who trot out the same tired eugenics talking points to argue that recent evolutionary developments have left Black people with lower IQs, making them naturally less successful than other races.[40] Scientists continue to disagree. In 2014, when human-biodiversity proponent and journalist Nicholas Wade published his book *A Troublesome Inheritance: Genes, Race and Human History*, a diverse group of 143 leading ecologists, biologists, geneticists, and others signed an open letter condemning it.[41] "We reject Wade's implication that our findings substantiate his guesswork. They do not," the group wrote.

So far, it seems that no amount of scientific evidence can stanch the flow of eugenicist thinking in US culture. Conservatives have used its lessons to justify cutting social spending and abolishing affirmative action. Trump's immigration bans reflected Murray's ideas too.[42] The problem is that eugenics and its modern incarnations are not truly based in science. They are, like all psyops, based on telling emotional stories and appealing to entrenched prejudices. Sometimes fighting them with fiction works better than fighting with facts. This was often Reed's strategy, and other speculative fiction writers have followed his example.

One such writer is N. K. Jemisin, a best-selling science fiction and fantasy writer who began her career as a psychologist. Her work often deals with the psychological impact of racism. In 2021, deep in the midst of the cancel culture debates, she wrote on Twitter, "White supremacy is a psyop." She would know, after years of dealing with online attackers whose rhetoric borrowed heavily from eugenics. In a noteworthy example, science fiction author Theodore Beale wrote a series of posts about Jemisin for the Science Fiction & Fantasy Writers Association (SFWA) in 2013. SFWA is a professional organization where Beale and Jemisin were both members, and his posts appeared on the organization's message boards as well as its official Twitter feed. Beale, whose nom d'internet is Vox Day, wrote: "There is no evidence to be found anywhere on the planet that a society of NK Jemisins is capable of building an advanced civilization."[43]

It was a classic eugenics argument, and Beale launched it into a professional forum to discredit a colleague. This is often what happens when a psyop is successful in a culture war: it enters a kind of rhetorical pipeline that carries it far from the public stage where *The Bell Curve* was launched. At the end of this pipeline, the psyop shapes interpersonal relationships at work and even at home. Many members of SFWA fell for the psyop, too. Maybe they didn't agree with him, but they thought he was simply elucidating a possible scientific interpretation of "genetic evidence." When Jemisin and others pointed out that his argument was racist, and inappropriate in a professional forum, Beale painted himself as the calm and reasonable one. Jemisin, he claimed, was an "ignorant savage" who was attacking him.[44] Again, we see the downstream effects of the false-rationality psyop, with Beale even using eugenicist language like "savage" and "ignorant" to describe a Black person who disagreed with him.

Jemisin dealt with Beale and other online trolls partly by writing stories like the Broken Earth trilogy, which exposes the inner workings of a racist industrial nation in the far future. Over the course of the novels, we discover that the true source of this nation's power is the labor performed by marginalized and sometimes enslaved "orogenes," people with the power to cause and prevent earthquakes and other natural disasters. It turns out that civilization cannot be maintained without a group of outcasts who literally hold everything together for their oppressors. But the books are not a cold assessment of a world broken by bad social policy. They focus on the life of Essun, a powerful orogene whose daughter has been taken from her—and Essun's harrowing, continent-spanning quest to find her child again. Jemisin's worldbuilding is awe-inspiring, but what stays with the reader long after putting the books down is the wrenching psychological realism of the traumas caused by a racial caste system. We see the upstream and downstream effects of psychological war playing out in Essun's life, and the effect is devastating. The Broken Earth novels won three Hugo Awards and became international bestsellers. Winning the Hugo Award for the final book in the series, Jemisin said in her speech:

This is the year in which I get to smile at all of those nay-sayers, every single mediocre, insecure wannabe who fixes their mouth to suggest that I do not belong on this stage, that people like me could not possibly have earned such an honor, and that when *they* win it's "meritocracy," but when *we* win it's "identity politics." . . . I get to smile at those people, and lift a massive, shining rocket-shaped middle finger in their direction.[45]

I was there in the audience at that Hugo ceremony, cheering along with the crowd of authors and fans as she held the award—shaped like a silver rocket—and delivered this parting zinger. Her novels, and the complex story of power and identity contained in them, had done more than a thousand op-eds ever could. They were a counter-psyop that stuck in people's minds, drowning out the eugenicists and their false rationality.

CHAPTER 5

SCHOOL RULES

When the weapons of psychological war come to the suburbs, we rarely hear about it. Every day, culture wars are fought out of the limelight, by people who do not have TV pundit gigs or the well-lit stages that come with that privilege. Sometimes when these wars erupt, their victims wink into media visibility for a moment, making it appear that both sides in the conflict are equally powerful. But that is rarely true, as high school journalism teacher Rachel Stonecipher discovered. In the fall of 2021, Stonecipher's fight with her suburban Texas school district became one of the most well-known examples of the anti-LGBT moral panic gripping the nation. When she lost her job for questioning the district's policies on LGBT student groups, it was shocking to the hundreds of parents and students who came out to protest. For anyone familiar with twentieth-century psyops, though, the pattern was all too recognizable.

Psyops become part of culture wars when a specific group of citizens is framed as a kind of foreign adversary. In the case of LGBT Americans, this practice goes back to the Cold War. As James Kirchick writes in *Secret City: The Hidden History of Gay Washington*, gays and lesbians had long been demonized as immoral—but it wasn't until the 1940s that they were classified as potential enemies of the state.[1] There were a lot of reasons for this shift. Perhaps the most high-profile one was a scandal involving Sumner Welles, a diplomat who served as Franklin Delano Roosevelt's undersecretary of state. Like many diplomats of his generation, Welles came from a wealthy family, and he had gone to Harvard alongside Roosevelt. Thanks to his connections, he quickly rose through the ranks to lead US policy in Latin America; when Roosevelt was elected, the new president wanted Welles in his cabinet. This aroused the ire of William Bullitt, US ambassador to the Soviet Union, who came from the same posh background as Welles and Roosevelt but felt that he hadn't reaped the benefits. In fact, Bullitt had been stewing over Democratic Party leadership for years because of a disagreement with Woodrow Wilson over how to negotiate with the Bolshevik government after World War I.

Bullitt wanted to make things uncomfortable for the Democrats, and in 1940, he found the perfect way to do it. A colleague passed Bullitt written reports from two Pullman porters serving on the presidential train, where they claimed Roosevelt's trusted adviser Welles had gotten drunk and propositioned them for sex. Bullitt began a secret campaign to oust Welles; he informed on Welles to Roosevelt and warned the president that homosexuals were easy targets for blackmail. When Roosevelt dismissed the Pullman porter reports as rumor, Bullitt tried another tactic. He passed the reports to Republicans in Congress and Roosevelt's cabinet, then leaked news of Welles's sexuality to the press. Fearing for his reputation and his life, Welles finally resigned in 1943. Ironically, Bullitt was himself bisexual and had sought a "cure" for it by going into treatment with Freud. Bullitt and Freud became close, partly because they both detested Woodrow Wilson, and they co-authored a book in the early 1930s called *Thomas Woodrow Wilson: A Psychological Study*. Unpublished until after Bullitt's death in 1967, it was about how President Wilson's international policies— poor ones, in Freud and Bullitt's opinion—could be traced back to his secret homosexuality.[2]

The Welles scandal had profound ripple effects. Bullitt's operation to mess with the Democrats had led to conspiracy theories in the US government. One was that homosexuals were vulnerable to manipulation by the nation's enemies. Testifying before Congress in early 1950, Senator Joseph McCarthy claimed that communists and homosexuals shared "peculiar mental twists." A week later the deputy undersecretary of state, John Peurifoy, confessed in a congressional hearing that the State Department had recently fired ninety-one homosexuals. It was the beginning of a purge now known as the Lavender Scare. By the end of 1950, the Senate had produced a report called *The Employment of Homosexuals and Other Sex Perverts in Government*. Senator Kenneth Wherry, an author on the report, said: "Only the most naïve could believe that the Communists' fifth column in the United States would neglect to propagate and use homosexuals to gain their treacherous ends."[3] A few months after Republican Dwight D. Eisenhower was sworn in as president in 1953, he signed an executive order that designated homosexuals a "national security risk." It was official: LGBT people were essentially enemies of the state, unfit to be public servants of any description.

THE RAINBOW STICKER PURGE

Sixty-eight years after the Lavender Scare, another public servant was about to be fired, for pretty much the same reasons that those ninety-one State Department employees were. It was August 30, 2021, and teachers and students poured back into MacArthur High in Irving, Texas, on a scorching hot day soon after summer break. A small suburb outside Dallas, Irving is known for its football stars and thorny local politics. Until 2010, its city council was entirely white, despite the fact that the city itself is one of the most diverse in the United States, with whites making up only 21 percent of residents.[4] But politics were the last thing on Rachel Stonecipher's mind as she ducked out of the heat and made her way to the classroom where she'd been teaching English for the past two years. She was excited about the new term, because she'd run a successful DonorsChoose campaign to get all the equipment she needed to start MacArthur's first-ever printed student newspaper. Swept up in first-month-of-school chaos, Stonecipher didn't notice anything out of the ordinary until she overheard students talking about being scared. Then she started to see messages on her phone from other teachers.

"One teacher was saying his door had been damaged," Stonecipher recalled, speaking to me by video from her home. That's when she realized what was wrong. Over the weekend before classes started, someone had gone through the hallways at MacArthur and used a sharp tool to scratch rainbow stickers off teachers' classroom doors. Roughly thirty teachers had the stickers, given out by the campus Gay–Straight Alliance (GSA) to show support for LGBT students. (Though the students and faculty at MacArthur called it the Gay–Straight Alliance, the national organization has changed its name to Gender and Sexuality Alliance.) "They were little two-inch stickers, rainbows and hearts, very subtle," Stonecipher explained. The stickers had been up for a year and a half, with permission from the school principal, and there had been no complaints from parents.

Stonecipher was one of a handful of faculty sponsors of the GSA. She told me that the work had made her more idealistic, especially after witnessing how homophobic students learned to accept their LGBT classmates. "I've seen people change in my presence. You need to have the imagination on both sides to figure out what is making people scared and respond to them." Stonecipher isn't fooling herself into thinking that everyone will come to like LGBT people, but "there's an in-between—you can have an opinion about the world but you have to be realistic and fair footed about sharing that opinion with other people." As she recalled talking to students about this topic, a smile crossed her face. "I always tell them, look around you—these other people aren't scared of gay people. There's no need to panic. See? Look at these other people. They aren't panicking. You don't need to panic either."

But that day, it appeared somebody had panicked. As Stonecipher and the other GSA sponsors tried to figure out who was responsible for the vandalism, the faculty received an email from the school's new principal, Natasha Stewart. Stonecipher frowned at the memory. "It said that per Irving Independent School District policy, there are no LGBT stickers permitted on MacArthur grounds."

That didn't sound right to her. She later texted a teacher she knew at another school in the district, asking if their rainbow stickers had been removed. "They hadn't taken [the stickers] down. So I knew there was no way that was a policy." Stonecipher decided to push back. The next day, she met with Principal Stewart, who continued to insist that there was a policy, though she didn't have a copy of it handy. "I was smirking, I will admit," Stonecipher said, and then her Texas accent thickened a little. "What [Stewart] was saying sounded so made up. I knew she was full of shit." When the GSA faculty sponsors emailed Stewart as a group, they demanded to see a policy from the district. None was forthcoming—at least, not yet. The principal simply sent them an email with a quote from Title IX, implying that it was justification for taking down the stickers because there was no equal representation of other groups. The GSA was mystified. What groups would seek "equal representation" in this case? Anti-LGBT hate groups? It made no sense, and they vowed to continue the push to get their rainbow stickers back.

It was, like many culture wars, a struggle over symbols. Those rainbow stickers were based on the LGBT pride flag, whose rainbow stripes are arranged in the same horizontal pattern as the red and white stripes on the American flag. Stonecipher recalled that MacArthur High teachers had many different national flags hanging in their classrooms, to show pride in their backgrounds or in the languages they taught. Other teachers posted religious iconography. A few months before the sticker ban, Irving ISD superintendent Magda Hernández quote-tweeted a motivational speaker who wrote, "I am here for God to refine me into what He wants me to be." Hernández replied, "And we are here to do His work! He places us where we are for a reason!"[5] But messages of support for

LGBT people were singled out for erasure. It was the Lavender Scare writ small.

Meanwhile, there was turmoil in Stonecipher's nascent journalism class. Some of the students wanted to investigate why the district had taken down stickers; they suspected anti-LGBT bias. Stonecipher agreed to let them look into it. "I told the newspaper students that it's OK to investigate whether teachers or administrators have homophobic intentions." The students set to work, which did not sit well with Stewart, who contacted Superintendent Hernández for help. On September 10, nearly two weeks after the stickers had been scratched off the walls, Stewart produced the promised policy document from the district, which restricted classroom decorations to ones that were "neutral in viewpoint."

However, the policy was dated August 30. That was the day when everyone had arrived to find the stickers already gone. It seemed to Stonecipher and the other GSA sponsors that the date discrepancy was the district incompetently backdating a policy to cover for Stewart's unauthorized destruction of the rainbow pride symbols. When Stonecipher pointed this out publicly, she was placed on indefinite administrative leave. That was on September 16, less than a month into the school year. One of her journalism students, Elle LeeAnne Caldon, wrote an article for the *Dallas Voice* about what happened next:

> Rachel Stonecipher, who questioned the removal of the stickers, was herself removed from the school—in front of her students. . . . Administrators escorted her out of her seventh period newspaper class. . . . Administrators have also stalled production of MacArthur's first-ever physical newspaper,

saying students are unprepared to produce it.... Instead, students ... were told to find a news article from any major news outlet, then spent three days in class "annotating" it, with 10 required annotations to mark "false information or facts." Without research into the issues concerned, students were expected to find "fake news" in the professional journalists' work they found online.[6]

The message was clear: the problem with Stonecipher wasn't simply her role in the GSA; it was her work on the school newspaper, which encouraged students to question school authorities. And the school was fighting back with propaganda borrowed from national debates over so-called fake news. The downstream effects of America's long-standing fixation on LGBT people as politically volatile (or "not neutral") were inundating MacArthur High.

At that point, the conflict had escalated way beyond stickers. It was now a battle over speech—specifically, whether teachers would be allowed to discuss LGBT identity with students. The principal announced that the GSA faculty sponsors could no longer discuss LGBT topics, which effectively ended the campus chapter of the LGBT support group. Then the school blocked access to the GSA website on the school computer network, along with three other LGBT rights organizations, including the Human Rights Coalition. The former GSA faculty sponsors repeatedly requested that these websites be unblocked, and got no response from administrators.

On September 22, the students had had enough. Hundreds of them covered their faces in rainbow stickers or carried rainbow flags and staged a walkout. The story was carried on local and national news, and Stonecipher's face was everywhere. For many people watching, it was hard not to feel empathy for a teacher who just wanted to teach journalism and make LGBT kids feel safe. Among Stonecipher's supporters was another Texas educator, James Whitfield, a Black teacher and principal at Colleyville Heritage High School, who had been put on leave a few months earlier,[7] when parents accused him of teaching critical race theory.[8]

After the barrage of news covering the protests, the school district finally issued its policy on the stickers to the public. School district leaders posted it on Twitter, while the students were marching:

> The district has developed guidelines to ensure that posters, banners and stickers placed in classrooms, hallways or offices are curriculum driven and neutral in viewpoint. . . . Irving ISD policy states that teachers shall not use the classroom to transmit personal beliefs regarding political or sectarian issues.[9]

Here, LGBT identity was being explicitly politicized, much the way it had been when Joseph McCarthy described it before the Senate in 1950. Needless to say, the stickers did not go back up and Rachel Stonecipher was never allowed to return to her classroom as a teacher. Around that time, Stonecipher remembered, she asked the other GSA sponsors if they thought she was receiving especially harsh treatment "because of how I look." A self-described butch lesbian, she had close-cropped blond hair and a fondness for suit vests. A look of frustration crossed her face as she recalled the experience. "Everyone thought [Stewart] was targeting me."

At this point, her fight wasn't just about stickers. It was about her job. There was only one final appeal she could make to the district, and that was to request a grievance hearing where she would make the case that she had been unfairly discriminated against. The hearing took place in March 2022, at the Irving Independent High School board meeting. Representing Stewart and the school district was attorney Dennis Eichelbaum, who argued that the issue wasn't about symbols of LGBT identity. "If teachers want to put up a rainbow flag in their classroom, they can do that," he claimed. "They can show support." But the rainbow stickers weren't sending a message of "support," he argued, but instead were misleading students into thinking that some spaces on campus were safer than others. He called the stickers "unsafe" and "dangerous," and insinuated that they encouraged illegal behavior that could get teachers fired.[10] Making a connection between LGBT symbols and illegal behavior put Eichelbaum squarely in the Lavender Scare tradition of suggesting that homosexuality leads to crimes against America.

THE FBI'S HOMOSEXUAL ERA

The school district's attorney was also playing on another long-standing myth about homosexuality, one that he could weaponize in an environment where LGBT people were already being painted as enemies of the government. It was the myth of the groomer. But authorities haven't always used the word "groomer," a term coined in the 1970s by law enforcement officers to describe child molesters who gain their victims' trust with kindness or gifts.[11] Back in the 1930s, the FBI used the epithet "sex criminal." FBI director J. Edgar Hoover seized on this term for homosexuality in the wake of a famous unsolved kidnapping case. In 1936, in the dead of winter, ten-year-old Charles Mattson was abducted from his porch by a man his terrified siblings described as "swarthy," with an accent.

Local authorities and the FBI swept the area for days, but found nothing. Ten days after his disappearance, Mattson's body was found by a hunter in the woods—he was naked and had clearly been beaten to death. Hoover brought hundreds of men in for questioning, but the perpetrator was never found. Still, Hoover used the crime to argue that the FBI needed to put homosexuals under surveillance, thus cementing in the public mind that there was no difference between LGBT Americans and murderous pedophiles.[12]

A military psyop often targets adversaries with threats of violence or imprisonment. Calling someone a criminal, especially one as odious as a pedophile, is one way to launch that kind of psyop. And that's exactly what Hoover's data-driven "sex deviates" surveillance program did. The FBI's focus on homosexuals continued to grow, aided by McCarthy's witch hunts in the 1950s, imperiling the lives of thousands of innocent LGBT Americans. This "homosexual as sex criminal" psyop also suggested that LGBT people were specifically a danger to children, which meant that upstanding parents should join the government effort to stamp them out.

In the 1970s, right-wing activist Anita Bryant founded Save Our Children, one of the first organizations aimed at parents who wanted to keep LGBT people out of public life. Bryant, a former beauty queen and pop singer, was a charismatic influencer who had been radicalized by anti-feminist movement leader Phyllis Schlafly. Bryant said she founded Save Our Children because the district where she lived in Florida had granted LGBT people housing and employment protections.[13] That meant it was going to be harder for employers to fire people for being gay. Sounding very much like Hoover, Bryant gave speeches about how gay people were "recruiting" children, and scoffed that asking for "gay rights" was the same as asking for "murderer rights."[14] California state representative John Briggs used a similar claim to justify legislation that would have prevented gay people from teaching in schools. The Briggs bill was defeated, but the myth of the gay pedophile lived on. In the late 2010s, the QAnon conspiracy crowd began to use the term "groomer" to evoke the same myth, and the word quickly made its way into political and legal speech. By 2021, when Stonecipher was caught up in the rainbow sticker war, the right-wing media was routinely referring to LGBT people as groomers.[15]

The same month that Stonecipher was put on indefinite leave, Florida governor Ron DeSantis signed the Parental Rights in Education bill. Critics dubbed it the "Don't Say Gay" bill, because it forbade teaching kids in K-12 classrooms about LGBT identities, or even mentioning a teacher's gay spouse.[16] DeSantis's rationale was that talking about LGBT identity was equivalent to bringing sexually explicit material into the classroom. By suggesting that LGBT-related topics were pornographic, legislators once again called on Hoover's nearly ninety-year-old story that LGBT people were sex criminals. DeSantis's Don't Say Gay legislation has spawned over a dozen copycat bills,[17] joining a wave of anti-trans bills banning drag performance and gender-affirming health care. Responding to pushback from the LGBT community and its allies, DeSantis's press secretary, Christina Pushaw, declared on Twitter that anyone against these pieces of legislation is "probably a groomer."[18]

Not surprisingly, this psyop has created a terrifying environment for LGBT people. Online and on the street, they receive death threats simply for being visible. Perhaps the most absurd example of this came during college basketball's March Madness festivities in 2023, when transgender social media influencer Dylan Mulvaney posted a sponsored video for Bud Light on Instagram. Mulvaney's brand is sunny and wholesome—she posts videos of herself offering friendly advice about transitioning, including makeup tips and positive affirmations for when times are hard. She's amassed nearly two million followers, but is hardly a political movement leader; she's more like the girl next door, amplified into stardom by Instagram and TikTok. Which is likely why Bud Light chose to partner with her, to boost their image among LGBT consumers. When Mulvaney posted the video of herself enjoying a Bud Light from a promotional can with her face on it, however, she was unprepared for the visceral attacks that followed.

Right-wing influencers online organized a boycott of Bud Light, but the responses to Mulvaney were personal. She received death threats and bomb threats. "What transpired from that video was more bullying and transphobia than I could have ever imagined," she told the *New York Times*. "I've been followed, and I have felt a loneliness that I wouldn't wish on anyone."[19] Mulvaney's experience is not uncommon. A 2021 study by the Pew Research Center showed that 51 percent of LGBT adults had experienced "severe forms of online abuse," compared to 23 percent of straight adults.[20] It's part of a weaponization pattern that begins with insinuating that LGBT people are a foreign adversary and ends with nondemocratic calls for their deaths—or an end to their livelihoods.

NO GAYS ALLOWED

Stonecipher and her colleagues were similarly targeted, especially after the media storm over the student protest, but that hadn't stopped their fight to be heard at the grievance hearing. As they sat in the audience, looking up at the stone-faced school board members, district lawyer Eichelbaum argued that teachers posting rainbow stickers were sending a message that kids should come to them to share sexual secrets. "The scary part about this is if a child comes to [teachers] with a concern, they have said they are not going to tell the parent about these issues," Eichelbaum told the board. He didn't need to use the word "groomer" because anyone paying attention to the media already knew what he meant.

Stonecipher's colleague Christine Latin, another faculty sponsor of the GSA, spoke up in support of the group. She described being traumatized when her mother forced her to go to gay conversion therapy as a teenager. Her voice thickened with emotion as she explained that sometimes LGBT kids need help at school that they can't get at home. Eichelbaum twisted her story into further evidence of grooming. "That's what the danger is," he said, referring to Latin's testimony. "The presumption that I can go to this teacher and I can share information and they won't tell my parents . . . because this is a safe classroom. And we can't have that." Eichelbaum warned that faculty sponsors in the GSA were "guiding" students rather than simply supervising them. And yet, as Stonecipher pointed out, it was the faculty's job to guide students during extracurricular clubs, just as a coach might guide them during sports practice. The "guiding" accusation made sense only in the context of a grooming myth. Again, the underlying message seemed to be that there was something dangerous about these students' exposure to LGBT adults and their allies—in the classroom and online.

Despite these claims of imminent danger, neither Eichelbaum nor the district could identify a single incident where a parent or student had complained about the stickers or the GSA. This lack of evidence mirrored events in another court case about LGBT rights, *303 Creative LLC v. Elenis*, which was playing out in the Supreme Court. In that case, the owner of a design studio called 303 Creative argued that she would like to make wedding websites but couldn't because her home state of Colorado would force her to do business with gay couples and compromise her Christian beliefs. Her concerns, like those about the GSA at MacArthur High, were purely hypothetical. 303 Creative didn't make wedding websites, and therefore no gay couples had ever asked the company for that service. Civil rights attorney Sherrilyn Ifill pointed out[21] that by taking the case, the Supreme Court had jettisoned the idea of standing, a legal concept in which a person can bring a lawsuit only if they have a stake in the matter. The only stake the plaintiff had in *303 Creative* was, as one legal expert put it, the right to hang a "No Gays Allowed" sign on its virtual shop window.[22] Similarly, the Irving Independent School District's case wasn't a response to genuine community concerns; it was about the right to discriminate against gay student groups.

Both bodies ruled in favor of discrimination. 303 Creative won its case, which meant certain businesses gained the right to refuse service to gay customers. Meanwhile, after considering the GSA sponsors' testimony and Eichelbaum's arguments for less than a minute, the Irving Independent School District board voted unanimously to uphold the ban on the rainbow stickers, and by extension to prevent any teachers from sponsoring the GSA.[23] The Lavender Scare psyop was alive and well, justifying the marginalization of LGBT people in a local school district as well as by the highest court in the land. And, just as J. Edgar Hoover would have wanted, homosexual lives were ruined. Stonecipher's indefinite leave was now definite. Though students and parents staged another protest, the district refused to let her keep her job.[24] Christine Latin, who described her terrifying experience with gay conversion therapy, quit at the end of the school year. One of the other teachers who sponsored the GSA switched schools.

Stonecipher sensed the undercurrent of groomer rhetoric in her case, and told me the great irony was that students in the GSA never talked about sex. "It was a place to take an intelligent approach to contemporary politics of LGBTQ identity," she said. "These are things conservative parents would want—an intellectual approach to who they are. If conservative parents are afraid of grooming and don't want their kids exposed to that, then they're barking up the wrong tree. Teachers are a good source of information. Better than TikTok."

AN EDUCATIONAL HOT SPOT

This isn't the first time MacArthur High School has been at the center of an international news cycle. In 2015, a fourteen-year-old aspiring engineer named Ahmed Mohamed brought a digital clock to school that he had put together at home. Because it made a ticking noise and was built on a circuit board that his teachers didn't understand, he was immediately arrested on suspicion of having a bomb or possibly a fake bomb. After police realized that the device was just a DIY clock project, the principal still suspended Mohamed for bringing a device to school that could be mistaken for a bomb. When his parents sued the school for discrimination, arguing that Mohamed, a Muslim, had been racially profiled, the incident went viral online. Though they lost the case, Mohamed became an overnight celebrity—the "Clock Kid," a culture hero for nerdy kids of color everywhere—and he even met with President Obama at the White House.

Perhaps MacArthur High has been a hot spot in the culture war over education because of its demographics—it's a majority-minority city outside liberal Dallas, with tremendous class diversity as well. That puts it at the crossroads between conservative and liberal forces in the nation. Still, this war isn't isolated to Texas suburbs. It's happening all over the United States, almost entirely at the local level.

Under the banner of "parents' rights," activists in cities and towns throughout the United States successfully lobbied to remove 674 books with LGBT themes from school libraries in 2022 alone.[25] Compare this with 2015, when there were only 275 challenges to books, and only a fraction of these were banned.[26] In Yorba Linda, California, school board trustee Todd Frazier won his seat by campaigning on a broad parental rights platform. He advocated taking LGBT topics out of the classroom, using this justification: "The classroom is not a place for social justice. It's for academics and teaching students to respect authority."[27] Frazier's comment sounds uncannily like a quote from one of the subjects profiled in *The Authoritarian Personality*, whose authors explored the psychology of fascists in the 1940s. Their research revealed that antidemocratic sentiment often began in childhood, among kids who were told by adults to obey orders rather than think critically about the world around them.

Else Frenkel-Brunswik, co-author of *The Authoritarian Personality*, believed that education could help combat propaganda by teaching critical thinking skills and exposing children to diverse perspectives. Her insight reveals why educational institutions are often a target in culture wars. Schools are a place where teachers are paid to shape young minds, to guide how children think and analyze the world around them. In the United States, public schools are also funded by the government, and they are where most Americans learn what it means to be a citizen of this country. So it makes sense that they're ground zero for anxieties about foreign influences.

A cursory look back at our history reveals that psyops targeting education are incredibly fungible. Today, advocates for Don't Say Gay bills and trans bans push for "parents' rights." Yet in the nineteenth century, legislators argued against parents' rights when it came to Indigenous children. During the Indian Wars, the US government took Indigenous children away from their families and taught values that contradicted their ancestral traditions. The justifications for residential schools were like the Don't Say Gay laws in reverse. Indigenous kids needed exposure to new ideas to help them progress, the government claimed. Parents had no right to set the curricula in these schools, nor even to visit their children on campus. Then and now, educational psyops harm children to punish—or appeal to—their parents.

Educators fighting back against school policies like the one at MacArthur High inevitably receive death threats. They lose their jobs, and they're criminalized as "groomers" by public officials such as Ron DeSantis, by local school boards, and by mobs online. That's because twenty-first-century culture warriors call for violence against their enemies, just as US military operatives would in a PSYOP product. But teachers aren't the only casualties. As many studies have shown, LGBT kids who are forced to hide their identities at school, or who face hostility for being out, are at a higher risk of suicide.[28] This isn't just a disagreement over stickers, or a democratic debate. Human lives are being destroyed.

Schools are places where we implant our hopes for the future in the minds of the people who will build it. When activists take away the right to discuss LGBT identity in school, they are participating in a larger project to eliminate LGBT people from the next generation of Americans. Refusing to teach kids about their history and culture is a way of erasing their futures.

Still, the war isn't over. Rachel Stonecipher doesn't want to leave her Texas town, and she isn't staying silent. After being fired, she created a podcast about gender identity based on her dissertation, which highlighted a diversity of perspectives—not just progressive ones. She told me her greatest hope was that her work would reach conservative listeners and help them see LGBT people as individuals with rights like everyone else in the United States.

CHAPTER 6

DIRTY COMICS

When school is the battleground in a culture war, sometimes educators have to leave academia in order to teach. That's what happened to psychology professor William Moulton Marston, who wanted to teach the world to respect women. But it wasn't until he created the Wonder Woman comic book that he found a classroom where he could do it.

Working at Harvard, Marston had made a name for himself in the 1910s by promoting a lie-detector test he'd invented. During World War I, he taught military psychology in the US Army, then spent the next decade rattling around various university psychology departments and conducting experiments on what he called the "psycho-neural mechanisms of emotion." In 1928, he published a book called *Emotions of Normal People*, co-written without credit by his partner Olive Byrne. He and Byrne suggested that most sexual desires were perfectly normal—even if society frowned on them—because humans were hardwired to want a wide range of sexual activities. There was no "normal," they argued, and it was toxic to teach people otherwise.

This argument came from personal experience as well as professional conviction. Marston was in a long-term polyamorous relationship with Byrne; his wife, Elizabeth Holloway, an attorney; and Marjorie Wilkes Huntley, a librarian.[1] Their polycule wasn't just some kinky lark: these relationships lasted Marston's entire adult life. He lived in a sprawling home with Holloway, Byrne, and their four children, while Huntley visited often enough to have her own room in the house. Inspired by the free-thinking women in his life, Marston began to layer feminism into his theories of emotion. But his family was deemed so scandalous that it got him booted from academia. One of his former colleagues at Harvard put a letter in Marston's file alluding obliquely to "rumors" about him. It was, as his biographer Jill Lepore notes, "the kind of thing said about homosexuals," and it was enough to get him blackballed from academia for life.[2] This setback seems to have solidified Marston's belief that he was in the psychological vanguard, and he continued to search for jobs that would allow him to normalize the idea of women's liberation.

Marston's career took a turn when Universal Studios hired him as a "mental showman" in 1928, to help predict where pictures were going and what people wanted from them. Hollywood had observed the way psychologists like Edward Bernays had revolutionized the advertising industry, and wanted some of that magic for themselves. Marston told execs that emotions should be "authentic," and that in romance movies, the "woman should be shown as the leader every time." After working on hit movies like *Frankenstein* and *Dr. Jekyll and Mr. Hyde*, Marston had created an odd but productive role for himself in the culture industry. Unlike Paul Linebarger, who drew a strict line between his psyops work and his fiction, Marston wanted fiction to serve as a vector for his deeply held beliefs about female power. In 1937, he gave a front-page interview to the *Washington Post* where he declared that "the next 100 years will see the beginning of an American matriarchy—a nation of Amazons ... and in 1,000 years, women will definitely rule this country."[3]

He managed to make that dream come true, at least in comic books. Max Gaines, who ran DC Comics, hired him in 1940 to create the character of Wonder Woman. Marston famously pitched the comic as "psychological propaganda for a new type of woman." His hope was that readers would be inspired by Diana Prince, an Amazon princess who could rule over men with love and truth. Indeed, one of Wonder Woman's greatest weapons is her Lasso of Truth; when she ensnares someone in it, they cannot lie. Marston explicitly rejected the Bernays approach to psyops, even going so far as to pit Wonder Woman against a supervillain named the Duke of Deception, who runs an ad firm. Marston wanted to empower women, not sucker them into buying cigarettes. He wanted to educate them about their histories, too. Each issue contained an essay about a real-life woman who had made important contributions to science and the arts, alongside an action-packed story about the Amazon who fought Nazis with her wits and superpowers. For Marston, propaganda was a progressive force, and like all propaganda, it contained an element of truth.

Wonder Woman immediately became one of DC's most popular characters, alongside Superman and Batman. Though Marston wrote the comic for only six years, until his death in 1947, Wonder

Woman's influence has continued unabated until the present day. But almost immediately, her adversaries weren't limited to the Duke of Deception, Mars (the god of war), and the misogynistic Dr. Psycho. Her greatest enemies were other psychologists, often working with the US government and the courts to convince the public that comics were filling kids' minds with filth.

KEEP YOUR BRAINS CLEAN, KIDS

In 1946, President Harry S. Truman signed the National Mental Health Act into law. He likely had no idea how it would be used against comic books. The bill allocated federal funding for research into mental health issues—especially those suffered by returning soldiers that today we would call PTSD—and to preventive therapies rather than institutionalization. The law was a long time coming, and was based in part on the progressive idea of "mental hygiene," a field of psychology that focused on promoting mental health through community services and education.[4] After World War II, however, mental hygiene became a kind of foil to brainwashing—it was the "good" form of mind control that could save people from falling prey to all kinds of menacing ideas.

Bolstered by support from the government, mental hygiene made the jump to popular culture. A new subgenre of documentary called the "educational film" entered US classrooms, giving kids mental hygiene lessons about everything from proper dating etiquette and gender roles to drug use and driver safety. Often produced by ex-GIs who had worked for the Office of War Information, where Paul Linebarger began his career in psyops, these films were both lucrative and ubiquitous. They were also, like the Wonder

Woman comic book, conceived from the outset as what film historian Ken Smith calls "tools of social engineering, created to shape the behavior of their audiences."[5] The difference was that mental hygiene films did it by threatening viewers with the specter of insanity caused by inappropriate behavior and crime—including J. Edgar Hoover's favorite crime of "sex perversion," aka homosexuality.

By the mid-1950s, experts viewed pop culture as a psychological battleground, a war between mental hygiene and dirty minds. Into the breach stepped a psychologist and moral crusader named Fredric Wertham, who published a best-selling book in 1954 called *The Seduction of the Innocent*, in which he argued that comics were the direct cause of violence, drug use, and homosexuality among young people. If classroom movies could prevent mental illness, then it stood to reason that comics could cause it. Wertham's book led to a national movement to keep comics away from children and teens. One immediate result was a restrictive editorial code, similar to the Motion Picture Code, issued by the Comics Magazine Association of America "for the protection and enhancement of the American reading public."[6] Among other rules, the code forbade representations of "sex perversion" and "indecent or undue exposure." Comics that touched on the topic of romance would always "emphasize the value of the home and the sanctity of marriage." While those rules were clearly aimed at *Wonder Woman* and other titles with female protagonists, the Comics Code was also focused on limiting what could happen in stories more generally. There would be no "glamorous criminals," and "in every instance, good shall triumph over evil." Also prohibited were scenes involving "walking dead, torture, vampires and vampirism, ghouls, cannibalism, and werewolfism." So many things were forbidden that it was almost impossible to stay within the code, especially because items like "undue exposure" were difficult to define.

For the next decade, Wertham fought comic books in lectures and in Congress, noting in a Senate hearing that "Hitler was a beginner compared to the comic-book industry. They get the children much younger."[7] As if it weren't already obvious that Wertham considered this a war, he had now openly compared comics publishers to the nation's most hated adversary. Comics, he suggested, weren't just threatening children's mental health. They threatened the very fabric of democracy.

Wertham's public advocacy for mental hygiene went back to the 1920s, when he began his career as an advocate for the poor and mentally ill. As an expert witness in the courtroom, he helped establish the idea that mentally ill people should not always be held responsible for their crimes. Most of the research he did for *Seduction* was at Lafargue Clinic in Harlem, the first psychological clinic in the predominantly Black neighborhood. Celebrated Black writer Richard Wright, long an advocate for psychotherapy, had spearheaded the project to build a clinic in his community. He and Wertham met after the publication of Wright's novel *Native Son*, which explores the destructive impact of racism on a young Black man's sanity. Wright was impressed that Wertham seemed to understand that poverty and racism can make life and mental health precarious.[8] And yet, Wertham ended up believing that the troubled children he worked with in Harlem were not suffering under Jim Crow[9] in a redlined city. Instead, they were being led astray by violent and sexual images in comics.

In the 1940s, comics were as ubiquitous in kids' lives as video games are today: at that time, more than 90 percent of children and 80 percent of teens in the US were reading comics regularly.[10] These statistics worried Wertham, who saw something "psychologically un-hygienic" in Wonder Woman.[11] As he wrote in *The Seduction of the Innocent*, she was a hero stronger than men, a "phallic woman," which he condemned as "an undesirable ideal for girls, being the exact opposite of what girls are supposed to want to be."[12] Describing a fourteen-year-old "delinquent" at his clinic who had "been in contact with some twenty-five social agencies," Wertham wondered why she couldn't overcome her "difficult social circumstances," including poverty and an unstable home. His answer? "Her ideal was Wonder Woman.... She was prevented from rising above [her circumstances] by the specific corruption of her character development by comic-book seduction. The woman in her had succumbed to Wonder Woman."[13] And the problem wasn't just Wonder Woman, according to Wertham. It was the representation of all women in the comic book. "They do not work. They are not homemakers. They do not bring up a family," he complained. "Mother-love is entirely absent. Even when Wonder Woman adopts a girl there are Lesbian overtones."[14]

At one point in *The Seduction of the Innocent*, Wertham makes a reference to Marston's contention that Wonder Woman offered a model of "advanced femininity" where women are equal to men. "If a normal person looks at comic books in the light of this statement he soon realizes that the 'advanced concept of femininity and masculinity' is really a regressive formula of perversity," he argued.[15] Having Wonder Woman as a role model was, to Wertham's mind, a cause of mental illness. The values she embodied were "unhygienic," leading women to believe they could work alongside men as equals—and even choose sexual partners who were not male. And thus, with one book, Wertham managed to gaslight a generation of young people who looked to the Amazon princess for guidance, truth, and a sense of hope. The mental hygiene psyop has the same built-in defense against criticism that the bell curve psyop does. Anyone who argued against Wertham was, by definition, mentally unfit—and therefore not trustworthy to advance an argument. Culture wars often produce these kinds of blanket diagnoses of whole classes of people, and these diagnoses are a difficult weapon to deflect.

Still, despite Wertham's best efforts, *Wonder Woman* did not go out of print, nor did her popularity decline—especially after the rise of second-wave feminism in the 1960s and '70s. Acknowledging the character's role as a feminist icon in the culture war, Gloria Steinem put Wonder Woman on the cover of *Ms.* magazine in 1972. A popular *Wonder Woman* TV series starring Lynda Carter gave the character a 1970s reboot, and she appeared in two blockbuster movies, in 2017 and 2020. Along the way, her character inspired countless other heroic women in pop culture, from Batwoman to the protagonists in an annual feminist science fiction anthology series that began in the mid-1970s with *Women of Wonder.*

Wertham's reputation has not stood the test of time as well as Diana Prince's. A recent investigation of Wertham's papers by University of Illinois comics historian Carol Tilley revealed that the psychiatrist fabricated, exaggerated, and selectively edited his data to bolster his argument that comics caused antisocial behavior.[16] Tilley's work was based on unprecedented access to two hundred cartons of Wertham's private papers at the Library of Congress, which were under seal until 2010. She pored over the

extremely detailed notes Wertham kept on interviews and sessions with the teens he worked with throughout most of his life.
Soon, Tilley realized that there were major discrepancies between
what Wertham recorded in them and what he wrote in *The Seduction of the Innocent.*

Some of Wertham's case studies in his book turned out to be
stories he'd heard secondhand from colleagues. A famous anecdote
about a Sheena-obsessed teen named Dorothy with a history of
violence came from another doctor. Tellingly, Wertham's account
glossed over the real-life violence that might have influenced Dorothy's behavior. Tilley writes:

> In the case notes, Wertham commented that the images of
> strong women reinforced "violent revenge fantasies against
> men and possibly creates these violent anti-men (therefore
> homosexual) fantasies. . . . Sheena and the other comic book
> women such as Wonder Woman are very bad ideals for them."
> Yet Wertham omits from *Seduction*—and seemingly from his
> analysis—a revealing story about Dorothy's everyday real-
> ity. In the case notes, she related an incident in which her
> aunt was accosted by gang members, taken to a rooftop, and
> robbed of less than one dollar.

Here we see Wertham refusing to acknowledge what Dorothy
told her case worker about the real-life traumas she suffered. He
believed that comics made her mentally unfit to explain what truly
ailed her.

When it came to violence inspired by comics, Wertham's greatest informant was a fifteen-year-old gang member named Carlisle.

Wertham had carefully transcribed interviews with Carlisle, and in the process of writing *Seduction* wound up attributing Carlisle's words to a succession of fictional young people. He's split into two different boys in one section, and Carlisle's words also find their way into the mouths of two more boys, ages thirteen and fourteen. So one informant became four. This was part of a general pattern where Wertham exaggerated the scope of his research. Though he testified to the Senate that he'd examined five hundred young people per year for several years, the archival evidence shows that for the ten years he worked at the Harlem clinic, only five hundred people under seventeen were admitted.

Tilley also found evidence in the Library of Congress papers that Wertham's observation that he'd seen children "vomit over comic books" was actually taken from a report by the psychiatrist's friend, the folklorist Gershon Legman. Legman was not an expert by any means, and ironically he was best known for books about dirty jokes and a guide to "ora-genital stimulation," or oral sex. But Legman had become an anti-comics crusader in the late 1940s, and that was enough for Wertham to include his anecdote as evidence. Wertham also claimed in *Seduction* that he'd seen comics for sale to children in stores where prostitutes peddled their wares. This was actually from an unverified report given to him by his colleague Hilde Mosse; Wertham himself never witnessed any prostitutes at comic book stores.

Though Wertham's influence had waned long before his lies and exaggerations came to light, the culture war over women's representation in comic books did not fade out. Instead, it moved to a new battlefield within the world of comic book creators and fans, where feminists were changing the scripts again.

"I THOUGHT WONDER WOMAN WAS PUERTO RICAN"

In the late 1990s, a comic book fan named Gail Simone noticed something odd. "I found that I most enjoyed reading about the girl heroes, or Superchicks. And it had been nagging me for a while that in mainstream comics, being a girl superhero meant inevitably being killed, maimed or depowered," she wrote. She made a list of 112 "superchicks who had gone down in one of those ways," including Wonder Woman, and was stunned. "When I realized that it was actually harder to list major female heroes who HADN'T been sliced up somehow, I felt that I might be on to something a bit . . . well, creepy."[17] Simone posted the list on a website she called Women in Refrigerators. The name is a reference to a notorious issue of *Green Lantern* that came out in 1994, at the height of the "grimdark" trend in comics, which foregrounded gritty violence. One of the high-ranking members of the Green Lantern Corps, Kyle Rayner, discovers that the bad guys have chopped up his girlfriend Alex DeWitt and left her remains inside his refrigerator. It's a horrific scene, and avenging her death becomes Kyle's primary motivation throughout that arc in the book.

After posting her list, Simone emailed a few dozen comic book creators—most of whom were male at the time—and asked what they thought. Their answers ranged from horror at the realization[18] to apathy because male superheroes are often killed in terrible ways too.[19] Still, no matter how people in the world of comics felt about Simone's list, it touched a nerve. In 1999, Women in Refrigerators was at the center of one of the first meme wars on the internet, galvanizing fans and creators to reexamine the role of women in comics. It also launched Simone's career. In the early 2000s, she was invited to write *Birds of Prey*, an all-female superhero team that included fan favorites Black Canary and Oracle. Her run on the comic inspired the 2020 *Birds of Prey* movie, which centered on Harley Quinn. Simone also became the longest-running female writer on *Wonder Woman*. As she said when she first compiled the "women in refrigerators" list, the world of comics was changing, and she was part of a new wave of women writers, editors, and fans who spoke out loudly when their heroes were forced to wear ridiculous cheesecake outfits, or to die in order to motivate male characters. In an interview shortly before she took the reins on *Wonder Woman*, Simone mused:

> Women respond strongly to . . . myths and fairy tales where the end is not always the prince and the knight come in to rescue them. . . . A lot of [people] really enjoy Birds of Prey because it shows that there's diversity there . . . different types of strength and different ways to stand up in that situation.[20]

One of those people was Vita Ayala, a nonbinary Afro-Latinx comics fan who loved Simone's *Birds of Prey* as a teen. As an adult, she became an editor at Marvel. Ayala also co-authored the first *Wonder Woman* series starring Nubia, a Black warrior who became queen of the Amazons while Wonder Woman was busy in Man's World. Hitting stores in fall 2022, it was called *Nubia: Queen of the Amazons*. I caught up with Ayala on video to find out what it's like to work in comics over seventy years after the birth of Wonder Woman. Growing up in the Bronx in the 1980s and '90s, there was no question in Ayala's mind that Wonder Woman was a person they could identify with. "I always thought Wonder Woman was Puerto Rican," they admitted with a laugh. "She's wearing a Puerto Rican outfit, with little shorts. She comes from an island of strong women. She looks like my cousin. She speaks Spanish sometimes—I remember her saying 'hola.' Finally, when I was sixteen, my mom said, 'No, she's Greek. She's involved with the Greek gods—her villain is Ares!'" Ayala shook their head, amused at the memory.

Despite their early identification with Wonder Woman, Ayala didn't always aspire to be a comic book writer. They started out wanting to be a teacher, and spent a semester in graduate school studying education. But they quickly grew disenchanted with institutions that "were not conducive to learning." They wanted to teach, but not in a system they saw as "pitted against" the very kids it was supposed to help. Like William Moulton Marston, who went from Harvard to Hollywood, they believed that superhero stories were a way to inspire kids outside the system.

"[Superheroes] don't have a moral with a capital M. But they are a way for us to talk about the things we find aspirational. To talk about hope in a way that's not too on the nose," they explained. That was especially the case with Nubia, a character they thought about very carefully with co-writer Stephanie Williams, a Black artist who has a longtime fascination with comic book history. The two of them decided that their first move would be to "modernize" the backstory of the remote Amazon island of Themyscira, where Nubia becomes queen. Nubia's origin in 1970s comics was not going to fly in the 2020s, they explained wryly. "Hippolyta prays for daughters, and makes one out of white clay who is good—that's Diana—and one out of black clay who was not so good. Nubia was raised on a parallel 'bad Amazon' island." As they discussed this origin story with Williams, Ayala realized that the story wasn't just racist but also undermined the idea that women have control over their own actions. The "white clay" Wonder Woman doesn't choose to be good but is simply built to be good, like an automaton. "It takes agency away from Diana," Ayala said. And obviously it made Nubia into a depressing stereotype of the Black woman who can't help but be bad.

Williams and Ayala gave Nubia a new origin story, where she climbs out of the magical Well of Souls on Themyscira along with many other Black and Brown women, all of whom have been saved from their oppressive lives in Man's World. After serving as a warrior on the island for many years, Nubia wins a contest of bravery and is crowned the Amazons' new queen. The question was, what would her powers be? Nubia doesn't have a Lasso of Truth like Diana, but she does have the power of understanding. "What is truth without empathy?" Ayala mused. "She can't compel you to tell the truth, but she can bring both of you to a place of understanding each other." She also has to learn that she matters to her people, which is why Ayala and Williams set the action on Themyscira—a place where Marston's Wonder Woman also spent a lot of her time.

In the story, Nubia must fight one of the Amazons' greatest foes, Medusa, who has escaped from a prison on the island. "We asked, what does it look like when a Black woman deals with that problem [of imprisonment]?" Ayala recalled. In the end, Nubia uses her power of empathy, and realizes that Medusa has been victimized, raped and turned into a monster against her will. "Understanding the perspective of the antagonist is part of being a hero," Ayala said. And there's another lesson folded into the comic as well: "Maybe jail isn't that great." They continued, "It's a lie to say you can create art without an agenda. It's about communicating, and you're communicating [your beliefs]." Marston imagined a world of powerful women, and Simone imagined a world where those women survived. Ayala and Williams imagined a world where women abolished prisons.

I asked Ayala if there are harmful tropes equivalent to "women in refrigerators" for Black and Brown characters in comics. Without hesitation, they replied, "Getting shot." As a writer and editor, they said, "I fight very hard not to have guns pointed at young Brown characters. I'm very aware of what is going on there. I try to allow young Black and Brown characters as much innocence as I can. I don't mean making them naïve. You can preserve their wonder and excitement and big emotions and not make [their stories] just trauma-based." Ayala and their wife recently had a baby, and as they spoke to me, Ayala gently cradled their newborn in a soft blanket, occasionally pausing for a quick nursing break. It made me wonder what kind of worlds that sleeping baby would discover in the pages of comic books written a decade from now.

CULTURE BOMB

Throughout her history, Wonder Woman has been used to ask a loaded question: What should we teach women about themselves? Does a proper young lady dream of commanding an army of Amazons and besting men in combat, or does she think exclusively about how to be a good homemaker to her husband? Psychologists Marston and Wertham argued that they were uniquely qualified to know, and came up with diametrically opposed answers. Over the decades, they were joined by politicians, feminists, fans, and corporate publishing executives with eyes on the bottom line—all of whom, in one way or another, called themselves experts on what makes a healthy fantasy for women.

Not surprisingly, the mental hygiene wars over Wonder Woman have surged and subsided with women's rights. The heroine burst onto the scene with Rosie the Riveter in World War II, but was demonized by Wertham in the conservative 1950s, when women were being encouraged to return to homemaker roles. Her relevance spiked again during the second wave of feminism in the 1970s, but her comic book was briefly discontinued during the conservative 1980s (the only time since her inception when Wonder Woman didn't have her own book). There had never been a movie starring Wonder Woman until 2017, and her cinematic debut was a smashing success at a time when the #MeToo movement against sexual harassment was brewing in workplaces across the country.

Conceived as "psychological propaganda" for a new kind of woman, Wonder Woman has always been more than a story. She is a weapon, a culture bomb that has changed people's minds about feminism. And she's inspired a predictable form of counterattack: the mental hygiene psyop, which frames Wonder Woman as an evil seductress, luring us into unhealthy behavior. This conflict goes beyond Wonder Woman, too; it has become a template for many of our bitterest battles over pop culture. Experts have accused video games of turning teens into the kinds of violent, unhinged delinquents that Wertham warned us about. Parents' rights groups demanding that LGBT books be taken out of school libraries are also relying on the same old mental hygiene model.

In the twenty-first century, the mental hygiene wars have been updated and recast as battles over "wokeness," a term that also implies an undesirable mental state. Creators including Vita Ayala have been targeted for coordinated online abuse for publishing "woke" stories about Black Amazons and LGBT X-men. These kinds of attacks have also targeted actors like Kelly Marie Tran, the first Asian American actor to play a major role in a Star Wars movie. Tran fled Instagram in 2017 after being bombarded by racist and misogynist harassment over her role as Rose Tico, a Resistance fighter in *Star Wars: The Last Jedi*.[21] Unfortunately, in this case, the psyop worked. Tran told the *Hollywood Reporter*[22] that she had to step away from acting for a while to protect her mental health. (She returned to Hollywood in 2021 to voice the lead in *Raya and the Last Dragon*.)

Some creators are able to steel themselves against the harassment, but it's never easy. When I asked Ayala about how they cope with the regular sniping they get on social media, they said, "I've been Black and queer my whole life. There will always be people who hate you for no reason." And then, sounding a lot like their character Nubia, they explained that they deal with the haters by trying to empathize with them. These people are lashing out because they feel bad about themselves, they said. Ayala doesn't want to make things worse by yelling back and heaping insults on them. "I force myself not to respond," they said simply. "That's my challenge. Not to say, 'You are small.'"

Anti-woke campaigns take aim at corporations too. Amazon took the unprecedented step of turning off user ratings for its 2022 series *The Rings of Power*, a prequel to *The Lord of the Rings*. Tens of thousands of people were "review bombing," giving the show one-star ratings, in an attempt to sink the series.[23] Their complaint? The series featured Brown and Black actors playing major characters, including an elf and a dwarf. Comments full of racist vitriol piled up on the show's review page, decrying the way this "woke" version of *The Lord of the Rings* wasn't true to the original vision of author J. R. R. Tolkien, whose heroic characters were white and largely male. Similar complaints had accompanied the attacks on Tran, because the original Star Wars movies featured white heroes (with the one exception being Lando Calrissian). Conservative commentator Matt Walsh condemned the *Rings of Power* series as "wokeist," while lauding all-white casts as "true to the original." His comments were part of a particularly puzzling moment in the discourse around *The Rings of Power*, when some fans claimed that the diverse casting wasn't historically accurate.[24] This actually isn't a new complaint—critics have been grousing about "historically inaccurate" people of color in fantasy video games for years.[25] One can read this response as a typically reactionary push for a return to traditional values of the past. But it's also an admission that culture warriors can't distinguish between history and fantasy. And they've had this problem for a long time. US psyops often take aim at history, as they did during the Indian Wars, rewriting it to feature an all-white cast.

While the creators behind targeted stories don't usually call their work "psychological propaganda," some are aware that they've made choices with political implications. In the case of *The Rings of Power*, the entire cast and at least one executive published an open letter supporting the casting choice for implicitly anti-racist reasons. "We're really proud of the cast that we have in the show. . . . We will not condone racism of any kind," Amazon's studio head Jen Salke told the *Los Angeles Times*.[26] We saw a similar scenario when *Barbie* movie director Greta Gerwig faced anti-woke backlash from men's rights pundit Ben Shapiro, who posted a forty-minute video condemning the movie's feminism. His millions of followers posted their own videos of burning their Barbie dolls. But Gerwig didn't budge: "My hope for the movie is that it's an invitation for everybody to be part of the party and let go of the things that aren't necessarily serving us as either women or men," she said.

Fallout from the Wonder Woman culture bomb continues in the modern war over what fantasies are appropriate and healthy for American minds. But there's another, deeper conflict that's being expressed in fights over popular stories. Paul Linebarger wrote in *Psychological Warfare* that there are two classes of propaganda: wartime and peacetime. "In war, the action sought by [the propagandist] is something militarily harmful to the enemy," he asserted. "[In] peacetime propaganda, the action sought is against the warmaking capacity of the audience—against war itself."[27] What is Wonder Woman but an icon of peace? Her greatest enemy is Ares, the god of war. Wonder Woman and her Amazon sister Nubia may be warriors, but their goal is to end conflicts using truth and empathy. Mental hygienists, however, design their psyops to harm and pathologize people they perceive as their enemies—whether those are what Wertham would call peddlers of perversity, or what Fox News would call wokeists.

Psyops are pernicious because they are designed to create a mental catch-22. If you notice the psyop, your own psychological health is called into question. In all the examples of culture war we've looked at, attackers portray their adversaries as stupid, criminal, and crazy—the kinds of people whose stories can't be trusted. It's hard to defend against a foe who convinces onlookers that you aren't being attacked or that, if you are, you deserve it. If you find yourself at the muzzle end of a psychological attack for long enough, it's hard not to question your own thoughts.

That's why the term "gaslighting" has become so popular over the past few years. It was the Merriam-Webster "word of the year" in 2022 because there was a 1,740 percent increase over 2021 in people looking it up on the dictionary's website.[28] The term comes from a play and movie of the mid-twentieth century, *Gaslight*, in which a woman's gold-digging husband tries to convince her that she's gone mad so that he can take control of her inheritance. He does it in part by toying with the gas lamps in their house, causing them to flicker, and then denying that it's happening when she notices. She starts to doubt everything she sees and hears, and fears that she truly is having a mental health crisis. Luckily, she has a friend who figures out what's going on and helps her uncover evidence that her husband has been deceiving her for financial gain.

The pathway to what Paul Linebarger called "psychological disarmament" begins when we find that friend—or when we are that friend. We have to work together to find the guy who is messing around with the gas lamps, and get the receipts to prove it. Unfortunately the problem that confronts the United States now is that the gaslighter is not just one guy. We are in an era of stochastic, decentralized gaslighting—and the traumas we suffer from psychological attacks began generations before we were born. Even if we as individuals get really good therapy, we cannot recover fully until our communities are also given the tools to recover. That's because the secret of psychological warfare is that it is not purely about vibes. It's about politics. And the only solution to political trauma is political transformation.

PART III

DISARMAMENT

CHAPTER 7

HISTORY IS A GIFT

We need to take the harm from psychological war as seriously as damage from total war. Whether the cultural battle is over ideology, identity, or history, we are wounded. People are hurt so badly they will never be the same; parents turn against their children and vice versa; some people die or commit suicide; and some are so badly neglected that they no longer have communities to support them. How do we put down our narrative weapons and start the process of rebuilding? It's worth thinking about a phrase that the United Nations teaches people engaged in peacekeeping after conflict: disarm, demobilize, and reintegrate, or DDR. DDR refers to the step-by-step process a nation goes through after war, with the goal of creating a sustainable peace between previously warring factions.[1]

During the first two steps, peacekeepers must destroy weapons and disband formal and informal wartime military groups. We've seen what disarmament and demobilization looked like after some psychological wars: the military dissolved and reorganized groups devoted to psyops as the Cold War wound down; the government restored sovereignty to some Indigenous tribes at various points in the twentieth century; and social media platforms created tools to track foreign-influence campaigns online after the 2016 election. Of course, there is no way for us to completely disarm and demobilize after psychological battle, just as you cannot guarantee a militia will hand over all its weapons after peace is declared. Indeed, many of these post-psywar actions were half measures at best. But they still sent a signal that the conflict was abating, and opened up a space in the public sphere for people to rethink the conflicts that tore the nation apart. The act of rethinking involves identifying the psychological weapons deployed in culture wars: framing groups of Americans as foreign enemies or "others," threatening adversaries with death, and lying. Psychological demobilization leads to changing the kinds of stories we tell, creating counternarratives that undermine the legitimacy of weaponized stories.

The final phase in the UN peace process, reintegration, is the hardest from a psychological perspective. After a total war, it means bringing former combatants back into civilian life, helping them to find jobs, social support, and in some cases, a new moral purpose. The UN recommends that former soldiers be given positions that make them stakeholders in the peace process, perhaps by offering them jobs rebuilding shattered cities or helping refugees. What would it mean to become a stakeholder in the pursuit of psychological peace? To answer, we need a definition of what psychological peace looks like on a mass scale. In the 1948 edition of *Psychological Warfare*, Paul Linebarger describes it as a state of "high national morale," bolstered by a government that improves education, provides food for children, builds public parks, and encourages "a fair-minded press."[2] The most important element of psychological disarmament, according to Linebarger, is freedom of movement across borders.[3] In essence, the architect of modern psy-war believed that peace breaks out when we restore government funding for social programs and tear down border walls.

Post-psywar reintegration is also a process of rebuilding our history so that it reflects the perspectives of everyone who lives in the United States. We cannot talk about intelligence without understanding how it has been weaponized by eugenicists, just as we cannot discuss pop culture without understanding how it has been shaped by moralists and revolutionaries. Psychological reintegration requires us to look frankly at our nation's past and acknowledge it. Only then can we begin to form new allegiances that will become the bedrock of a new public sphere.

REMAPPING THE PAST

The fallout from the Indian Wars is still radioactive, especially in the West. But the Coquille tribe in southwestern Oregon is mapping a way to the future by excavating its past and presenting it to the world for everyone to see.

Coquille tribal chief and anthropologist Jason Younker's story has many beginnings. One is in the 1850s, when the Coquille and Coos tribes—his ancestors—signed treaties with US government forces, who promised them federal aid in exchange for some of their land. It started again in the 1930s, when the US government recognized the Coquille as a tribe after declaring them extinct in the

1880s. And the story started *again* in 1989, when the federal government restored the tribe's status a third time, after terminating it in 1954. "I'm one of the last generations to have been terminated and restored," he told me by video from his office at the University of Oregon at Eugene. "I was born a terminated Indian, and twenty-two years later I became an Indian—even though I lived in the same place as my grandfathers' village." One thing never changes in the stories he tells: the place where it all happened, a windy stretch of Pacific coast riddled with rivers that snake across sandy flats and through the thickly forested mountains. Today, the land is occupied by a small city called Coos Bay. But in the 1850s, the region was home to dozens of tribes, including the Coos, Coquille, Siuslaw, Tolowa, Umpqua, Siletz, and more. Many were signatories to treaties with the United States, but "before any of the treaties could be ratified, militias went around and started burning villages," Younker explained. "So General Joel Palmer said, 'To move [the Indians] from harm's way, we are going to remove them before the treaties are ratified by Congress.'"

Tribes on the coast fled to a safer location, a lozenge of sandy wetlands at the southern tip of a bay. "That was South Slough, Coos Bay, where I grew up," Younker said. At that time, the only legal way his ancestors could remain near their homelands was to assimilate, often by cohabiting with white settlers. "The Indians, those who were cohabiting, lived in Charleston, which is right there on South Slough," Younker said. "Charleston really is the slums of Coos Bay—that's how bad it was for Natives living in their homelands. I was the 'dirty Indian kid' at the end of the street on Battle Flats where the Indians lived." Battle Flats isn't labeled on maps of South Slough today, but I found the spot that Younker was describing at the end of two long streets that stretch south out of Charleston and dead-end next to the silty edge of a shallow river.

Unmapped places and terminated identities haunted Younker's childhood. "When I was growing up, and I look the way I do, there's no getting around people asking, 'Are you Mexican? Hawaiian?'" He gestured at his face, indicating his brown skin and straight black hair. "I'd say, 'No, I'm Indian.' Or I'd say, 'I'm Coos,' or 'I'm Coquille.' And they'd say, 'There are no Indians here.'" He frowned. "If you asked your family members why we aren't Indian, they would say, 'They lost the map.' As a kid, you wonder what that means. They lost the map? But you quit asking because when people [say] 'they lost the map,' there's just horrible pain behind it." He paused and looked at me. "That is psychological warfare."

It was also a mystery that Younker was determined to solve. As he got older, he learned more about why so many people in his tribe were upset about the map. Back in the 1850s, he told me, General Palmer signed treaties on behalf of the United States with the tribes in the region and put them in an envelope. In a second envelope he stashed a huge map of the Oregon Territories, which showed all the locations of the reservations the tribes had agreed to. "Well, the map got lost, so when Congress looked at the treaties, they said, 'We don't know what you're talking about.'" Younker sighed. Without a map claim, the tribes were chased off their lands by militias. The map finally turned up in the 1880s, but by then it was too late. "The government said, 'Well, there's no more Indian problem so there's no reason to ratify these treaties. It goes down in Coquille history as 'they lost the map.'" Though the government's official stance was that there were no Indians in Coos Bay, they nevertheless sent a number of Indigenous children to boarding school in

Pennsylvania. This familiar psyop from the Indian Wars, in which Indigenous people are seen and erased at the same time, is why white people said to Younker's face that there were no Indigenous people in Coos Bay.

JASON YOUNKER GOES TO WASHINGTON

Younker went to college and studied to be a teacher. He had just gotten his first job when the Coquille tribal council recommended another path for him. This was in the early 1990s, during the congressional hearings over whether the remains of Kennewick Man should be given to scientists or sent back to the tribes to be reinterred. "They said we could really use an anthropologist in the room," Younker remembered with a chuckle. "And when the council 'recommends' something, it means 'go and do.'" It turned out to be a turning point for Younker and his tribe. While he was earning his PhD in anthropology at the University of Oregon, his mentor George Wasson, also a member of the Coquille tribe, organized a special trip for himself and several graduate students to the National Anthropological Archives and the National Archives in Washington, DC. Their goal was to learn everything they could about Coquille history as well as that of neighboring tribes. Writing about it later, Younker recalled:

> At that time, we were told that we shouldn't get our hopes up "as the Coquille were a very small Indian tribe and there probably wasn't very much information to be recovered," and in this light, the Smithsonian generously agreed to pay for the copies of whatever we found. . . . Much to the amazement of

our Smithsonian hosts, at the conclusion of our 1995 research, we had copied nearly sixty thousand pages of historical, anthropological, military, and government documents relating to the Coquille and neighboring Indian nations.[4]

Clearly, the museum workers were not prepared for what Wasson thought of as "an archival reconnaissance mission." But the research team knew exactly what they wanted, and how deep the rabbit hole might go: they came armed with over seven hundred keywords—from the names of tribes to the names of anthropologists who studied them—to guide their quest through dusty boxes that had lain untouched in a museum basement for decades.

Younker and his younger brother, who was also on the research trip, made a beeline for the Cartographic National Archives in College Park, Maryland. Listed in the catalog was a huge map from the 1850s. "When they rolled it out we knew exactly what it was," Younker recalled. "That was the lost map!" They quickly made a special copy for themselves.

As someone who has done quite a bit of work in archives, I kept wondering about that moment when Younker, Wasson, and their colleagues went to the museum staff and asked for all those copies. Today, it's typical to see researchers in archives with phones or digital cameras, quickly saving the yellowed pages to the cloud. But in the 1990s, everything had to be xeroxed by hand—and xeroxing a delicate, oversized map would have been expensive on top of being a huge pain in the ass. "Was that map one of the things they xeroxed for free?" I asked Younker. He caught my drift, and we both shared a laugh. "Yes it was!" We laughed again, and for an instant I could feel the pleasure of a psyop undone. The Coquille students had been offered free copies in part because the authorities at a US government museum believed, like generations of white settlers before them, that almost nothing remained of Indigenous culture. Not only did Coquille anthropologists prove them wrong, but the National Archive actually kept its promise to pay for sixty thousand pieces of evidence that dispelled the "vanishing Indian" version of history. It didn't make up for generations of abuse and violated treaties, but it was something. The government was relinquishing a psychological weapon by putting the truth about tribal history back into the hands of the people it was stolen from.

Younker and his colleagues dubbed their nascent archive the Southwest Oregon Research Project, or SWORP. When they returned to the council together they unveiled the map. They told their story about growing up hearing about how the map had been lost—and with it, their tribal identity. "People wept," Younker said. "It was like you were holding the one thing that proved you were Coquille, but it was also the reason why you weren't Coquille." The map now belonged to the tribe, and they could decide what should be done with it. Since that time, the Smithsonian has digitized the map so that researchers all over the world can see a high-resolution scan of it—including the rips and stains that tell the story of its bumpy history.[5]

A COPY BETTER THAN THE ORIGINAL

I drove up from San Francisco to visit the SWORP archives in Eugene, and spent two days on the road in northern California and southern Oregon. My mind on missing maps, I tracked my progress using an app called Native Land, which geolocated me in overlapping tribal homelands of the West Coast: Miwok, Pomo, Cahto, Yurok, Tolowa, Chetco, Coos, Umpqua, Siuslaw. It was late winter, and fat clouds rolled over the green valleys and redwood forests; in the distance, sheets of rain turned the mountains a dark, fuzzy gray. Rivers flowed alongside and under the road, often connecting with ocean. Rocks the size of skyscrapers reared out of the surf, covered in hardy scrub, orbited by calling birds. Rivers, towns, mountains, and campgrounds took their names from tribes and their languages. Once the app showed me who lived in the places where I drove, I found Indigenous presence everywhere: there were tribal community centers and clinics, casinos and shops. But I needed a map made with Indigenous data to see it.

Gaining entrance to the Knight Library archives at the University of Oregon in Eugene was a little more mellow than getting badged into the Hoover Institution Archives. All the librarians wanted to know was which items to bring to my desk from the fourteen boxes of material I'd reserved. Of course, I started with the maps. There were two boxes of them, and a kind archivist helped me unroll the oversized papers carefully, pinning their edges down gently with soft beanbags. On the back of each one was a stamp: "COPY The National Archives, Civil Works Map File." Carefully, I went through them until I found it—the lost map, called simply "A Sketch Map of the Oregon Territory." Tied with pink twine, its edges had gone soft with handling. I stood over it, trying to read the spidery handwriting that had divided the land into a puzzle of reservations and cessions. This was the old-school 1990s Xerox that Younker described to me, with tiny lint shadows from the document glass visible in the white spaces.

Forgetting myself for a second, I turned to the archivist and whispered excitedly, "Look! These are the Xeroxes!" She gave me a weird look and went back to the circulation desk. Apparently researchers aren't usually excited about Xerox copies, which makes sense—generally archives hold original documents. But that's what this was, in a sense: the original documentation of a very important copy.

Along with the maps, a lot of the early historical information in SWORP comes from government anthropologists working with the military. They ranged from the oldest anthropological reports on the local tribes in the mid-nineteenth century, to salty correspondence between government agents and the War Department about the cost of sending Indian kids to distant residential schools in the 1930s. For the most part, these documents tell a story of rescue anthropology, where people swooped into war zones and forced relocations, trying to learn as much as they could about the languages and traditions of shattered Indigenous communities. I found fragments of the Coos and Umpqua languages in a thick book full of blank spaces for "words, phrases, and sentences to be collected," organized into categories like "persons" and "dwellings." These blank books were created by J. W. Powell, a military veteran who ran the Bureau of Ethnology at the Smithsonian and gave them to everyone working in the field.

Powell believed that all cultures shared the same basic structure, and thus considered it reasonable to ask every Indigenous tribe the same exact questions. Not surprisingly, this often resulted in bad data collection. For example, he set aside a whole page for words about "gens," a nineteenth-century anthropological term for people connected through male ancestors. But the Coquille and many neighboring tribes were matriarchal, and there was no place in Powell's fill-in-the-blank books for an entire realm of Indigenous social experience. Meanwhile, under the section on "religion," Powell asked for translations of "God (the supreme ruler—the white man's God)," and then left a mere eighteen lines for the researcher to record the entirety of the tribes' own beliefs, histories, and stories. George P. Bissell, who collected Coos and Umpqua vocabulary, recorded the word for the white man's God and left all the other lines blank (luckily, other ethnographers collected some Coos stories, which are included in the archive). Many anthropologists did not use Powell's book; they were required only to collect 180 words on a worksheet before moving on to the next tribe.

These SWORP documents are packed with words, stories, and pictures from Indigenous history, but they also reveal plainly how agency leaders primed their teams to ignore key aspects of tribal culture. They also show how anthropology was marshaled against Indigenous groups during and after the Indian Wars. Just as Cold War psyops used the language of science, Indian War psyops used anthropology. New fields of academic expertise emerged in the United States, partly to explain what was happening to the Indigenous people and European settlers living alongside each other. "Historians" and "anthropologists" became paid professionals, working with governments to document and justify genocides whose effects are still being felt today.

POTLATCH FUTURISM

The SWORP archive is not just a record of what has been lost. It also contains documents from the late twentieth century, when

Younker and the research team revived an important Coquille tradition and started a new chapter in tribal history.

When Younker and his colleagues returned to the University of Oregon with thousands of documents, they decided to found their archive by combining Coquille traditions with anthropological practices. They would hold a potlatch ceremony to give the data away—the first Coquille potlatch in over 150 years. Many tribes in the Pacific Northwest traditionally held regular potlatches, ceremonies that establish alliances and consolidate power through lavish gift-giving. As Younker wrote in his master's thesis, nobody is sure why the Coquille tribe held potlatches, but it was likely for similar reasons. With the arrival of white settlers and their violent destruction of Indigenous communities, Coquille potlatches became small, private affairs. Eventually people stopped holding them altogether. It seemed fitting to reclaim the potlatch tradition at the same time that they reclaimed parts of their stolen history.

In 1997, the research team held a potlatch where they presented SWORP to the University of Oregon and eight other tribes. The event is meticulously chronicled in the SWORP archives: there are pictures and video of the ceremony, as well as a thick folder containing notes from all the meetings they held to plan it. Correspondence among the tribes is preserved, as well as Younker's master's thesis about the potlatch. This aspect of SWORP is part of a new practice that scholars call Indigenous data sovereignty[6] or, as Indigenous activist Vine Deloria succinctly put it, "the right to know."[7] The idea is that Indigenous people should control documents relating to their own tribal histories, much the way any nation would control its own museums and archives. At the Coquille potlatch, history itself—and the record of that history—became a gift. As Younker put it to me:

> We need to use this information to write a more accurate history. That's going to be a long, slow process. But we're making progress in showing people that, yes, this is why Coquille are still here, and these are some of the reasons why we look the way we do. Our traditional culture is shattered and our language is gone, but that does not negate that we are descendants of the Coquille.

Today SWORP is one of many Indigenous archives in the United States,[8] some of which are being digitized to make them even more accessible.[9] These archives take the fantasy out of history, often by collecting primary sources from the very organizations that tried to hide or ignore Indigenous claims to the land. What Younker and his colleagues ultimately created through their archival work was a narrative, a local history of colonization of the lands of the Coquille, Coos, Umpqua, Tolowa, Klamath, Siletz, Confederated Tribes of Grand Ronde, and many more, as told in the voluminous correspondence among US scientists, representatives of the military, and government. And the narrative reaches into the present with the record of the potlatch that Younker and his colleagues organized. SWORP is an ongoing effort; in 2006, Younker's former student David Lewis (Confederated Tribes of Grand Ronde) completed a third SWORP project to digitize records that covered all of Oregon.[10] The digitized collection remains in the possession of the Coquille and Grand Ronde tribes, "pending a future potlatch event," as Lewis put it.

SWORP could also be used to defend against future attacks from the US government. Younker said he still worries about his tribe being terminated again. Maybe the government won't use the word "termination," he said, but he's very aware that the tribe's fortunes could change quickly and dramatically. "We are in a good position to educate people right now because they are open to it, but in the 1990s, when gaming was coming along, they would say Coquilles are 'just playing Indian.' What if we open a marijuana dispensary and it's controversial? What's going to make people turn on us again?" Through SWORP, Oregon tribes have access to reams of evidence showing their historical connection to the land, and history is the cornerstone of sovereignty. That truth may help protect their land claims, whether in a court of law or in a culture war over the legitimacy of their identities. But there is a more personal, psychological dimension to SWORP as well. Younker mused that "the best thing about the SWORP archives is finding the things you knew to be true in your head." It's harder to gaslight someone when they have receipts from hundreds of witnesses that corroborate what they know.

Archives are more than a defense against psyops. They are a commitment to a new story about identities made whole in an ongoing psychological peace process. Younker concluded, "Really what we want to say to our next generations is that you are Coquille no matter what you look like, no matter how you behave." Out of boxes of carefully organized data, the tribes of Oregon have built fresh alliances and a narrative that can carry them forward into a sovereign future.

CHAPTER 8

DEPROGRAMMING FOR DEMOCRACY

Psychological disarmament requires a very different strategy when you're doomscrolling social media all day, eyeballs melting under the barrage of half-truths, memes, news, entertainment, and state propaganda. The 2016 election demonstrated that it's hard to track an online psyop unfolding in real time because there may be several random connections between the operatives and their audience. Because online psyops campaigns move so quickly, we have to be ready for them in advance. It's a bit like disaster preparation. We need skilled first responders at tech platforms, moderators and safety managers who can spot propaganda outbreaks and put them out before they explode. But we also need to create firebreaks, technical features that can slow the spread of weaponized information.

PROPAGANDA DISASTER PREPPING

In 2020, I witnessed an online influence campaign so devious that I could not stop thinking about it—in fact, it inspired me to begin researching this book. The reason I found it so compelling was that it was a two-stage psyop: first, the unknown operatives spread a wave of disinformation; next, they spread a second wave that was designed to inoculate people against any efforts to debunk the first wave of disinformation. It was incredibly intricate and complex, and here's how it went down. Like many Americans, I had been getting most of my news about the Black Lives Matter protests on Twitter, following eyewitness reports in various cities. One night I started to see posts on Twitter claiming that the entire DC area was in lockdown and there was a blackout.[1] Posts with the hashtag #DCBlackout began piling up in my feed, and at first they seemed credible. They appeared to be from ordinary citizens reporting from the ground.

But then I noticed some red flags that made the #DCBlackout reports seem suspicious. First of all, many people posting under the hashtag used the exact same words to describe what was happening, as if they were copy-pasting from a script. That was definitely a signature move of operatives who didn't have the time to come up with more organic-sounding content. But then came the capper: posts with the #DCBlackout hashtag started sharing a new message, which was that law enforcement was blocking cell phone access to prevent them from sharing the truth. That's when I knew #DCBlackout was a ruse. How could people be posting on their phones from the scene of the protests if their cell signals were blocked? Despite this logical inconsistency, rumors of the blackout spread quickly, resulting in five hundred thousand tweets with the #DCBlackout hashtag.[2] Some included fake images of a fire near the Washington Monument, which came from the (fictional) TV series *Designated Survivor*.

Reputable news sources moved to counter the blackout rumors. I remember seeing tweets from NPR and *Washington Post* reporters with selfies proving that they were in DC, surrounded by well-lit buildings and streetlamps.

And that's when the second wave of the psyop began to inundate my feed. Hundreds of posts with a new hashtag, #DCSafe, started to pop up, denying that the DC blackout was happening. Unlike the tweets from news reporters debunking the blackout, these tweets were clearly copy-pasted by psywarriors or maybe bots. They all used the exact same, quirky phrasing:

> yeah . . . as someone seeing #dcblackout trending, who lives and works in the DC metro area, and who has friends telecommuting into DC rn. . . . . This hashtag looks like misinformation. "No social media from DC" because we were asleep. Stop scaring people. #dcsafe[3]

It was a psyop designed to look like a psyop. People on Twitter quickly noticed the duplicate tweets coming from a wide variety of accounts, and called them out as fake. But why would a group of psyops agents want their targets to figure out that they were being fooled? The answer is that they didn't. By making the "debunking" tweets from #DCSafe so obviously inauthentic, the operatives also cast doubt on the real tweets from journalists at NPR and elsewhere. The #DCSafe operation made it seem like some shady group was trying to cover up what was happening in DC, and that the mainstream media was in on it. Anyone debunking #DCBlackout looked suspicious by association, as if they were part of a psyop. It was a brilliantly nefarious move: an influence operation to arouse fear over a fake blackout, and then to arouse fear over a fake cover-up of the fake blackout. Though I was troubled by how quickly the misinformation had spread, I couldn't help but admire the complex narrative structure of the hoax—especially the way it was so meta, with the #DCSafe tweets calling attention to themselves as a psyop in order to reinforce disinformation from the first wave of #DCBlackout tweets.

The DCBlackout/DCSafe operation was an example of what disinformation experts call "coordinated inauthentic behavior." Though nobody has identified the perpetrators of this particular psyop, it was certainly coordinated by operatives—possibly foreign—and then amplified by regular people tuning in to the hashtag. The first tweet to use the #DCBlackout hashtag had only three followers, but then it got amplified by accounts with greater reach and went massively viral in a matter of minutes. I was left wondering how that happened, and so quickly.

It turns out I wasn't the only one. A few weeks after the hoax, a paper came out in *Science Advances* that suggested a way we might deal with this kind of influence operation in the future. A team of researchers described how they had created an automated system for identifying influence operations on social media and predicting what they'll do next. Princeton University researcher Meysam Alizadeh told me that the group wanted to make a public dashboard showing "what's happening on social media and whether there is coordinated activity sponsored by foreign states." They trained a set of algorithms to spot the telltale signs of so-called influence campaigns. Working with datasets released by Twitter and Reddit, the group concentrated on troll activities originating in Russia, China, and Venezuela between 2015 and 2018.

Soon the algorithms had learned to spot distinctive propaganda patterns. Alizadeh and his colleagues set them loose on datasets that contained some troll posts and some "control" posts from typical users to see how they would fare. After several tries, the algorithms were able to predict most of the time whether or not a post was from a troll. The Venezuelan trolls were easiest to identify, with 99 percent accuracy on some tests. When it came to Chinese and Russian trolls, the algorithms got it right between 74 and 92 percent of the time.[4] That wasn't perfect, but it was a good start.

The real question is, how do you separate real social media nonsense from fake, when the fake accounts are constantly discussing new topics? Alizadeh said the answer is to train these troll-seeking bots on new data every month. Using the previous month's activity, he and his team try to generate accurate propaganda weather reports for the next month. This kind of work is sometimes called "prebunking," and it's been shown to work. However, it's always going to be an arms race—especially as operatives start jumping from one platform to another, or using AI like ChatGPT to generate fake stories and propaganda posts.

AN ELECTION WITHOUT HOCKEY STICKS

I wanted to know what the future of that arms race would look like, so I got in touch with Alex Stamos, the former chief security officer at Facebook who spotted the 2016 election psyops campaigns as they unfolded. I've known Stamos for many years, and I remembered running into him at a conference for computer hackers in Las Vegas right after he'd accepted the Facebook CSO job. We were at a party full of computer security experts, tech policy wonks, and journalists like myself, and people kept peppering Stamos with increasingly drunken questions about why he was going to a company known for its privacy and security blunders.[5] "I'm going to be the canary in a coal mine," he told us. "If you hear about me quitting Facebook under mysterious circumstances, you'll know why." At the time I shrugged. I knew his intentions were genuine, but I also knew that corporations have a way of sucking people into doing things they never thought they would. But he was as good as his word at that late-night party. Facebook PR types were vague about the reasons for his exit from the company, but as soon as Stamos could speak freely, he did. It's largely thanks to him and his team that the company admitted Russian operatives ran psyops on Facebook during the 2016 election. When Stamos quit, he made a public statement about how troubled he was by Facebook's data-collecting practices, and their unwillingness to take a side in debates over humanitarian issues.[6]

Stamos was the founding director of the Stanford Internet Observatory, a nonpartisan, interdisciplinary group of researchers who advise government and industry about misinformation campaigns online, as well as other trust and safety issues. For the 2020 election cycle, the Observatory joined a coalition of other research groups called the Election Integrity Partnership (EIP) to track election misinformation on social media. The EIP built a simple online reporting system that allowed election workers, cybersecurity experts, academic researchers, and nonprofit citizens' groups to file "tickets" reporting election dis- and misinformation as it flew by on eight different social media platforms. After intensive analysis, the EIP concluded that online influence campaigns were a driving force behind the 2021 insurrection at the Capitol.[7]

I met Stamos at an Arab street-food spot in San Francisco, where we talked about the state of digital psyops over a bowl of hummus served with cardamom-spiced coffee. I asked him what had changed between the presidential election cycles in 2016 and 2020, both of which included significant digital propaganda. He said one obvious difference was the source of influence operations: in 2015, a significant number of operations were foreign, but in 2020 most were done by Americans to Americans. The 2016 campaign taught the big platforms like Facebook how to spot and shut down most of the foreign election meddling. However, as Stamos put it, they hadn't figured out how to stop "Trump and his allies priming everyone to believe the election would be stolen." As a result, there were stochastic influence operations coming from all sides. Ordinary citizens, primed by political leaders to see conspiracies everywhere, spread disinformation as eagerly as paid propagandists.

"Do you remember SharpieGate?" he asked excitedly. "When people said, 'My pen is bleeding through the ballot and that will invalidate my vote'?" He was referring to an incident during the presidential election in Arizona, where Republican voters began posting on Twitter about how they had been given Sharpie pens while Democratic voters hadn't.[8] The story was bunk—Arizona election officials provided ample evidence that their voting machines could read ballots marked with Sharpies—but Stamos wasn't interested in that part. He and the EIP team were focused on how the rumor spread across social media and then erupted into the mainstream. It started at the top, but then it spread laterally among ordinary voters. "People got triggered, because they were already primed with the message that the election would be stolen. And a lot of people start saying, 'I also voted with a Sharpie,'" Stamos recalled. "And that's when Fox News called Arizona." Trump's team had been expecting a win, and immediately cried foul. At that point, SharpieGate erupted across social media.

It became what Stamos called "an open conspiracy," where people kept adding more supposed evidence from the ground: pictures of Sharpies, blurry ballot images, and more. Paul Linebarger would have instantly recognized open conspiracies as a form of worldbuilding, where people generate stories out of suggestive hints dropped by operatives. Influencers on Twitter picked up the initial Sharpie rumors and amplified them with the SharpieGate hashtag. Trump's children tweeted about it, and a QAnon candidate for governor in Arizona, Bryan Masche, announced there would be a protest at the capitol, where people should bring their Sharpies and "hold them high."[9]

It was a viral explosion pattern that the EIP team saw repeatedly. While it seemed as if everybody was suddenly talking about SharpieGate, the reality was that "a huge percentage of disinformation was spread by twenty accounts on Twitter," Stamos said. The EIP team dubbed these accounts "superspreaders."[10] Their information-sharing pattern reliably created what Stamos called "hockey stick graphs," where audience numbers abruptly swerve upward like the blade on a hockey stick. "A few people pass it around, then a [superspreader] retweets it, and the whole thing goes hockey stick." The result is that a handful of influencers can create the illusion of a widespread problem, by cherry-picking a few tweets and inspiring their millions of followers to share them. When a piece of information is suddenly everywhere on social media, that doesn't make it true—in fact, that could be a sign of an influence campaign.

To prevent election misinformation like SharpieGate, Stamos suggested, the public needs to interrupt what experts call an "influence operation kill chain." The kill chain is a set of steps—or links in the chain—that operatives go through as they escalate their influence operations. In the case of the IRA on Facebook, for example, operatives started by creating divisive political ads. That was the first link. Next, they used those ads to steer true believers to the IRA's Facebook pages devoted to fake political groups. Ultimately, the IRA activated an audience that amplified their messages by sharing posts and eventually going out in person to protests. At any point in that chain, the public and social media platforms can step in and stop influence operations before they infect the public sphere with confusion.[11] We can shut down fake pages, or prevent misinformation from going viral.

In many ways, the EIP's ticketing system is a microcosm of how the influence operation kill chain can be interrupted in a democracy. First, EIP formed a coalition of groups who represented experts and the public, and then they created an easy way for them to share information. The EIP included election workers, cybersecurity experts with the federal government, and academics, but also civil society groups like AARP, which represents retired people, and the National Conference on Citizenship, a seventy-year-old nonprofit devoted to civic engagement. Representatives from all of these groups spent the election season creating tickets about misinformation on platforms including Facebook, Twitter, Nextdoor, TikTok, and YouTube—then sending these tickets to trained EIP workers. Some tickets referred to large numbers of posts with disinformation, and others only one. From September 3 to November 1, the group logged 269 tickets. Things heated up in the days leading to the election: from November 2 to 4, they logged 240 new tickets. Most of the tickets chronicled threats of violence intended to suppress voter turnout, while others flagged misleading information about how to vote and false claims about election legitimacy.

Dozens of people at the EIP analyzed and fact-checked each ticket, working with their partner groups to decide how to address the misinformation. Sometimes they would issue a propaganda weather report, alerting social media platforms when they found a specific influence campaign such as SharpieGate. They also posted public alerts on the EIP website. That broke another link in the influence operation kill chain, because the EIP was sharing what it learned with the public to help stanch the flow of falsehoods. Plus, the EIP kept lines of communication open between all the groups involved—from election workers on the ground to citizens' groups and social media companies—so that everyone was on the same page about what constituted misinformation and where it was coming from.

After the presidential inauguration, the group wrote up their report, including basic guidelines to help social media companies deal with election misinformation in 2024 and beyond. Hopefully, this report will make it easier for the public to recognize and interrupt influence operation kill chains next time. The EIP suggested that the federal government focus on misinformation as a part of election security, developing standards for alerting media and the public to active influence campaigns. Social media platforms would have to become more proactive in their efforts to label misinformation, they said, using consistent messages when labeling dis- and misinformation. Once the government and social media companies had come up with rules for handling influence campaigns, they needed to stick to them. Accounts that spread misinformation should be shut down, the report suggested; but if that wasn't possible, superspreaders' posts could be sandboxed, or not allowed to spread through viral sharing. The problem, Stamos admitted with a grimace, is that labeling, banning, and sandboxing require cooperation from the companies that run social media platforms. And most platforms don't want anyone messing with the secret sauce they use to algorithmically generate their flow of content. Some, like X (formerly Twitter) and Reddit (owned by Advance Publications, which also owns Condé Nast), are already making it much harder for future versions of the EIP to do their work—both have shut down data-sharing programs that helped researchers judge the authenticity and provenance of posts.

Ultimately, the biggest takeaway from the EIP's report was that communication lines need to be wide open between local governments, election workers, industry, and citizens' groups. "The most important thing is accurate messaging from officials," Stamos said. "One of the core things we were trying to do was alert public officials about misinformation so they could [tell constituents] what was a rumor and what was true. We would say someone is saying the polls are closed, and maybe you should send out a message that they are still open. That's not censorship. It's addressing a lie that people are telling." Unfortunately, courts have been making it more difficult for governments and social media platforms to work together on efforts to stop disinformation. Citizens need accurate information about how to vote. And that will happen only if the government works with social media to clear away the disinformation chaos in a systematic, open way. The best way to do that, the EIP found, was to work with a large staff of human beings who could analyze the disinformation. Though automated propaganda weather reports like the one created by Alizadeh and his team are helpful, Stamos emphasized that humans had to be the final arbiters of what was disinformation and what wasn't. They understood the context of posts that would stump AI.

Still, the rise of AI apps like ChatGPT made Stamos wonder whether it would be possible to build an entire fleet of propagandists controlled by one person with a herd of chatbots. "The answer is maybe," he conceded. That's another propaganda disaster scenario we'll need to prepare for. If AI creates an even denser fog of misinformation, human moderators will be even more crucial. They'll be able to distinguish between violent threats and democratic debate and separate the deliberate lies from honest mistakes.

SLOW MEDIA

We also need to rebuild social media systems to prioritize human choice rather than algorithmic chaos. I talked about this idea with Safiya Umoja Noble, a UCLA professor who studies algorithmic bias and wrote the influential book *Algorithms of Oppression*. She likes to compare doomscrolling on social media to other addictive behaviors, like smoking. Smoking is a good parallel because many regions now restrict where people can smoke and require companies to put warning labels on cigarettes. You can still light up a cigarette, but there's friction involved in the process. She imagined regulators using anti-smoking laws as a model for social media regulations. For example, companies could be forced to limit the notifications that platforms use to draw people back into looking at their socials.

No more cute messages popping up on your phone, drawing you back into Meta products like Instagram and Threads. Limits could also be placed on "for you" or "you might like" suggestions that keep people clicking. That would mean fewer algorithmically suggested videos in your YouTube and TikTok feeds, tempting you into five more minutes with the app.

Another possibility would be to slow down the circulation of content on the platforms. "Maybe it will be more like newspapers or snail mail," she mused. "You submit something [to YouTube] and it doesn't show up the next minute. Maybe we'll upload things and come back in a week to see if it's there." She acknowledged that this would be a significant, qualitative change and would require a "completely different business model." But she pointed out that "there are other kinds of slow business models in entertainment. It takes a long time to make films and shows—even journalism. There is some value in slow."[12]

Her ideas are starting to catch on with former Twitter addicts who left the platform in the wake of Elon Musk's takeover in late 2022. Many moved their accounts to Mastodon, a social media platform with some of the same features as Twitter but where posts don't circulate as quickly. There are a few technical reasons for this. One is that Mastodon accounts aren't all in one centralized location. Users open accounts on a specific server, often devoted to a particular interest like science or art, and these servers are federated with each other via a protocol that delivers posts from one to the next. The collection of all websites and platforms using this protocol is referred to as the Fediverse. Information transit in the Fediverse works much like email, which also uses a protocol that sends your mail between, say, Gmail and Outlook. Posts on

Mastodon rarely do a viral hockey stick because server operators choose whom they want to federate with, and they can block servers that are a source of misinformation. Even when servers are federated, posts don't instantly appear on all servers at once. Indeed, some posts never leave their servers, while others hop across the Fediverse slowly, shared between individuals on different servers. Reading posts on Mastodon feels like Twitter in slow motion.

Noble told me that social media companies could also put the brakes on sharing our data. People need to know where our content is going as well as where it comes from. Facebook sometimes acts as a data broker, selling profile information to advertisers and other third-party companies. When people post, they should do it knowing whether their photos will be used to train facial-recognition algorithms or their words consumed by large language models like ChatGPT. They should understand whether their personal profile is being aggregated and sold to advertisers or political operatives who want to target people like themselves. Knowing who might use our information will introduce yet another layer of friction and might make us pause before posting our cute selfies and clever manifestos.

Over the past few years, the social media landscape has been undergoing a gradual transformation. Tech journalist Taylor Lorenz called it "the death of mass media."[13] People are fleeing the larger platforms such as Facebook for places like Discord, Slack, and group chats, where small groups gather by invite only. These are spaces where a quip or opinion cannot explode into everyone's phones, simply because posts there are designed to stay within the community, shielded from the broader public. We're flocking to apps that make social media feel more like visiting a pleasant public square rather than a hellscape of garbage fires and angry weasels. Our future media could target smaller audiences while also becoming slower..

We need to supplement these changes with new approaches to the algorithms that control what we see online. Companies could measure engagement in morale boosting rather than doom-scrolling. Indeed, Facebook ran an experiment in 2014 where they tweaked the content algorithm to promote stories that fostered positive feelings about other people.[14] I'm not suggesting we should manipulate people into passive acceptance, or force everyone into a "love thy neighbor" mode. Instead, we would foster a democratic public sphere where people are encouraged to disagree without threatening one another's lives or jobs. As security technologist Bruce Schneier put it, "We need to become reflexively suspicious of information that makes us angry at our fellow citizens."[15] Future systems of media could help us talk to one another again, by slowing down and considering our words.

BUILDING A BETTER WORLD, ONE STORY AT A TIME

"I could not think of a way to have a good future with the internet as it exists today," Ruth Emrys Gordon told me from her home office near Washington, DC. Like Linebarger, Gordon leads two lives: as a researcher, she analyzes online disinformation at the University of Maryland and government agencies; and as science fiction author Ruthanna Emrys, she writes about fantastical forms of war and social conflict. I called her up to talk about her recent novel *A Half-Built Garden*, an alien first-contact story where humans have created a better way of communicating online using what she calls "dandelion networks." It wasn't easy for Gordon to let go of today's technology, even in her imagination. "I like the internet," she admitted. "I like having a stream-of-consciousness telepathic feed. But I don't see how that's compatible with the societal relationships we need. So I wrote about an internet that has been broken into smaller networks with stronger protections between them to slow down discourse a bit and provide incentives for people to think about the value and accuracy of what they were sharing." Her thought experiment in the novel is based on what she's learned over years of analyzing what has gone wrong in the digital public sphere.

In her novel, humanity has to manage Earth's ailing ecosystems or, as the alien visitors warn, we will die. She imagines a democratic debate about how to care for a watershed as it blooms across the dandelion network, calling upon only the people who live within the watershed or affect its health. Everything in the environment is measured and remeasured, so that the participants' conversations are fact based, without the confusion of propaganda. Algorithms aid them by surfacing moments of agreement and reasonable compromise and by making sure that minority voices are heard. There is conflict, and it's difficult. But nobody calls for the deaths of their neighbors. "It's really about the structures we put together to facilitate social relationships," Gordon explained. She meant both her novel and the internet as we know it. "Our communications have to be structured somehow. Even when we're getting together in person, [there's a difference between] having a meeting and gossiping." The problem right now, she believes, is that we've lost those basic communication structures, and we're mired in a fog where we don't know the difference between meetings and gossip, information and opinion. Or between psychological war and democratic debate.

Gordon's work feels like a hopeful continuation of Linebarger's. After earning a PhD in cognitive science, she studied ways to defend Americans against what she calls "malign influence" or "cognitive attacks." Fiction gives her the freedom to imagine alternate scenarios in fantastical or future civilizations that echo those on Earth today. Unlike Linebarger, she's open about the connection between her two lives as researcher and author. "There's a value to speculating about doing things differently," she said. "One of the tools of science fiction is to help us not see the status quo as inevitable." In this way, she echoes a number of authors who write what are sometimes called "useful fictions" or "applied science fiction." Malka Older, author of the Centenal Cycle, focuses on a future global democracy run by a coalition not unlike the EIP that fights digital misinformation. Older is a humanitarian aid worker and disaster researcher, and her writing often deals with how to rebuild failing democracies and transform our structures of communication. In her recent book *The Mimicking of Known Successes*, Older imagined how humans might rebuild our society by settling in the upper atmosphere of Jupiter, forming small towns and cities strung along planet-encircling railroad tracks. In university labs and the halls of government, the people of Jupiter struggle to regrow Earth's lost ecosystems, in the hope that one day we will return to the planet that gave birth to us.

The field of applied science fiction is growing. Peter Singer, author of *Wired for War*, is another applied science fiction author who began his career writing critical commentary about military strategy. In 2015, Singer and co-author August Cole published the novel *Ghost Fleet*, about how a future war with China might unfold kinetically and psychologically. He and Cole went on to found a small firm called Useful Fiction, which teaches military commanders to use tools borrowed from storytelling in order to imagine possible scenarios. This, they believe, helps the military make better decisions in complex situations.

Quartz magazine used applied science fiction as the foundation for a speculative multimedia story about how to build sustainable communities in the wake of catastrophic climate change. "Welcome to Leeside, the US's First Climate Haven" is about Leeside, a former Rust Belt city in the Great Lakes area, which becomes a receiver city for climate refugees. The story includes a healthy dose of real science and engineering documents, alongside concrete policy ideas for reshaping people's relationship to limited natural resources.[16] Applied science fiction is also a way to think through our responses to health crises. Former medical researcher Naseem Jamnia wrote about how to handle a public health crisis caused by magic—and poorly funded hospitals—in their fantasy novella *The Bruising of Qilwa*. And Karen Lord, a former diplomat from Barbados, speculated in her book *The Blue, Beautiful World* about alien technologies ushering in a new age of diplomacy on Earth after powerful extraterrestrials contact humans and help them join a galactic-scale United Nations.

These authors join many more who are actively trying to offer their readers an alternative path, one that leads us out of the fog and away from psychological war. As Gordon put it, we need stories because they offer us something to work toward. Still, she cautioned, we can't get there without agreeing that some ideas should be "disallowed" in the public sphere. "We have to get to a point where we have the type of healthy disagreement and political discourse that allows a thriving democracy . . . while also disallowing [questions like] 'Is climate change something we should solve?' or 'Should queers exist?'" Both questions are part of psyops that rely on climate disinformation or the notion that LGBT people should be criminalized or worse. Gordon hoped that in a future public sphere, we "agree about who is a person" because everyone in a democracy is a person. "In many places we've forgotten you can have disagreements while still keeping your eye on the real problems. We can argue about housing policies and disagree strongly about how to deal with homelessness—but we must agree that [the unhoused] are people."

She imagined that a state of psychological disarmament would require us to meet in person more often, the way people often do at the house where she lives with her wife and children. "We have a nice porch and have a tendency to feed people," she said, laughing. She said her neighborhood is extremely diverse and "we disagree about a lot of things, but we still say hi to each other when they walk their dogs and still bring food trays when they're sick or have a baby." It's one thing to say this, but quite another thing to see and feel it in a story. In her novel *A Half-Built Garden*, we witness a world where people care for a watershed whose needs are addressed as if it were a member of the community. The dandelion network brings those future people together in an America where we do not reach consensus by threatening one another with death—instead, we promise one another a better life.

CHAPTER 9

PUBLIC SPHERES OF
THE FUTURE

t's one thing to imagine a future world with aliens, or a fantasy city dealing with climate change. It's quite another to conjure a better public sphere in the world we live in now, where our history and media have become theaters of psychological war. After all the research I did for this book—some of which left me immobilized with grief—I realized that we already have a perfect metaphor for a rejuvenated public sphere. The public library.

In his book *Palaces for the People*, sociologist Eric Klinenberg describes libraries as a key part of our "social infrastructure," the fabric that keeps our communities whole. "People forge bonds in places that have healthy social infrastructures," he writes. "Not because they set out to build community, but because when people engage in sustained, recurrent interaction, particularly while doing things they enjoy, relationships inevitably grow."[1] Libraries are also safe places, offering free access to the internet, help with schoolwork or résumés, and public bathrooms. But these descriptions fail to encompass how personally transformative it can be to enter a library.

Megan Prelinger, founder of the renegade Prelinger Library in San Francisco, has never forgotten her first library experience. She was an early reader at three years old, and she went to the Eugene Public Library in Oregon with her dad. "When my dad came back from Vietnam he was pretty damaged—he had seen a lot of bad war stuff, and was outside the workforce because he was almost catatonic for a while after his service," she told me. "He and I were very close because his PTSD brain was harmonized with my three-year-old brain. We'd go to the children's section of the Eugene Public Library and lay on the beanbags there and just read. That's what we would do all day, when he was my caregiver and my mom was in school." She paused, pushing her dark bangs out of her eyes, remembering. "It was a safe space away from trauma. We could just lie there and be together, safe and unbothered." She described how she felt perfectly at ease among the tall stacks of books, warm and cared for. And when she grew up, she wanted to create the same kind of space for other people who needed it.

SOMETIMES YOU NEED TO HIDE

The Prelinger Library is slightly to the west of downtown San Francisco, on the second floor of a refurbished warehouse space that sits on a heavily trafficked corner where leather bars and nightclubs are interspersed with furniture stores and vacant lots. Access is via freight elevator, and the library's massive double doors are at the end of a hallway wide enough for a forklift. When I first walked inside, shortly after it opened in 2004, I felt like I was in an ancient cathedral. The space is dominated by metal bookcases that tower fourteen feet overhead, and the ceilings are much higher than that. Light pours in through tall factory windows made up of dozens of rectangular glass panes fitted into metal grids. Researchers try not to make too much noise as they clang up rolling ladders to access the highest shelves. Most of the items in this library exist nowhere else—either because they are one-of-a-kind art projects or because they were deemed too ephemeral and unimportant for mainstream libraries. There are collections of zines and underground histories of environmental activism. Boxes of *TV Guides* from the 1970s and '80s sit next to thick leather-bound volumes of congressional proceedings, engineering manuals, and Cold War books about brainwashing.

Prelinger, author of *Another Science Fiction: Advertising the Space Race, 1957–1962*,[2] is fascinated by the intersection of science and propaganda. She often sits up front at the computer, working with her husband, Rick Prelinger. He's a film historian and archivist, creator of the Prelinger Film Archive, a digital repository of industrial and educational films that includes titles used in the mental hygiene movement of the 1950s and '60s. Over the years, Megan and Rick had amassed book and periodical collections that grew as local libraries consolidated their inventories in the 1990s, selling off what was considered unimportant. "I was curious what US culture would look like if you mapped it based on what was discarded or free," Megan said. She began that mapping project in college by picking up free magazines at gas stations, but later found herself rescuing complete sets of old trade publications from libraries. I've browsed them at the Prelinger Library, and it's easy to get sucked into weird things you never knew existed, like a magazine for funeral parlor directors from the 1960s.

Megan worked with volunteers to create a special organizational scheme for the library, grouping the collection by subjects that include forestry and land management as well as the history of media, Indigenous life, and prejudice against youth. As the library website puts it: "This arrangement system classifies subjects spatially and conceptually beginning with the physical world, moving into representation and culture, and ending with abstractions of society and theory." When I asked Megan what she hopes people will experience in the library, her answer echoed Klinenberg's idea of social infrastructure. "If somebody is trying to come to terms with being a human, there is an instinct to hide, but there's also an instinct to explore. And in the library those two don't contradict each other. Hiding in the stacks is a form of discovery." She said she's not against social media, but doesn't feel that it's as conducive to sharing ideas as browsing in the stacks. "Physical books are easier to pick up and put down. They don't pull you in the same way as electronic media. The library is a lower-stimulus environment." She frowned slightly, then seemed to think aloud. "How often is it publicly discussed that people thrive better in lower-stimulus environments?" In the early twenty-first century, when people aspire to multitask their way through ten-hour workdays, practically never.

The Prelinger Library does outreach to local schools, and they get a lot of students coming through the space. It's made Megan painfully aware that school libraries are typically used as computer labs rather than repositories for printed material. "One thing about younger visitors—they've never even seen a roomful of books," she said. "They have an emotional and creative freakout when they encounter it. They've seen books depicted in media, but not in a library." She smiled. Watching young people go through that "emotional and creative freakout" gives her hope, especially because the Prelinger Library offers fellowships for artists who want to keep the freakout going and produce work inspired by what they find on the shelves. Libraries like Megan's—a nonprofit that isn't affiliated with a government or school—are one way to combat the book bans and library closures that are on the rise in the United States right now. They may also be our best hope of holding on to what she calls "a safe space, a welcoming space, a public park of ideas."

Public libraries are struggling, but they still provide free access to knowledge for everyone in the United States. They are packed with books, newspapers, and internet kiosks offering facts and diverse opinions. But they are not thrown together haphazardly in a pile that we have to sort through on our own or perhaps with the aid of an extremely confused algorithm. They are organized by librarians like Megan Prelinger, people who have been trained in the not-so-simple art of finding and contextualizing information. Without librarians, the library is merely a bricks-and-mortar version of the internet: a bewildering, overwhelming collection of ideas presented without structure or meaning. In a sense, the librarian is a content moderator, someone who offers guidance through the stacks of fantasies, thought experiments, scientific facts, and spicy opinions.

As physical spaces, libraries are models of what Gordon called structured communication. Often they contain at least one special-use room where people can hold public meetings, author readings, or after-school study sessions. But the rest of the library defaults to silence. They are places where we come to be alone with our thoughts, to learn from what other people have said without anyone else yelling in our ears about it. We need that silence. It's a space to make our own decisions, to evaluate what we as individuals actually think rather than what influencers and operatives tell us is right. When we immerse ourselves in the silence of the library, we learn the most fundamental defense against psyops. *Our minds belong to us.* And all those books and other media that surround us, waiting for an audience, were fashioned by minds just like ours. Maybe we don't agree with them, but in the public sphere of the library we can respect their psychological sovereignty just the same.

JUST PLAIN INFORMATION

Stories are weapons. They are also, as the Coquille potlatch attests, gifts of peace. Still, they must be subject to democratic forms of moderation and structure if we don't want to be overwhelmed by information chaos. What exactly would stories look like in a world after psychological disarmament?

I sat down at the large wooden table that greets visitors as they enter the Prelinger Library and asked Rick and Megan what they thought. Could they imagine a world without propaganda? They couldn't, and neither could I. There will always be propaganda, and there will always be operatives who want to poison us with paranoia and threaten us with death. But, Rick conceded, there might be such a thing as good propaganda, or a story that doesn't hurt us. That kind of story, Megan added, would be focused on repair, growth, and change. Or it might be something like a PSA. "It would have to be evidence based," Rick pointed out. "Maybe just plain information like 'Don't put your hand in the fire.'"

I looked around at the books stored high over my head, many of them devoted to seemingly mundane subjects like building an industrial threshing machine or preparing a road for paving. Nothing fancy. Just information. Perhaps, when we stop brutalizing one another with clever tales, we will be left with something as plain as a PSA. At that point, maybe our fiction will transform as well—free, at last, to be pure flights of fancy instead of artillery in somebody else's war.

Achieving psychological peace doesn't always require us to tell new kinds of stories. Instead, it involves understanding how many of our social interactions are shaped by the stories we've heard. It's about recognizing weaponized stories when they come flying at us, instead of accepting them as factual or unquestionably good. Public policies, fictional tales, and educational materials are all stories that can become psyops, aimed at cowing us or changing our behavior. We need to be suspicious of demands that come wrapped in glib narratives.

Still, there is an even more difficult task that lies before us: *we must end this war.* That means trusting one another enough to put down our psychological weapons. And it means acknowledging one another's right to be alive, in the United States, as sovereign minds that do not require cleansing, disciplining, or civilizing. To do it, we'll need epic adventure tales that celebrate our commonalities, and philosophical treatises that remind us of our shared past. We must change ourselves, together, and our stories can light the way.

ACKNOWLEDGMENTS

This book started as a short manifesto that I intended to write quickly in early 2020, but events conspired to make it an intense research project that took over two years. There were many months when the weight of this traumatic national history almost paralyzed me, but luckily I found voices of hope. Thanks go to the many experts who spoke to me during that lost time, often by video. Despite everything that was going on, they turned on their cameras and welcomed me into the cramped, makeshift home offices where many of us worked during the pandemic. And of course, thank you to Megan and Rick Prelinger, whose radical, tranquil library is where this book began and ended. I have tried to represent all of your stories to the best of my ability, and any errors are my responsibility. Thanks to Matt Weiland, my discerning editor, who has a gift for rethinking narrative structure—and is always ready to talk to me about midcentury Marxism, punk rock, and environmental science. Many thanks also to Huneeya Siddiqui, for keeping the manuscript moving, and to the rest of the gang at W. W. Norton for always being excited about books that veer off the beaten track. My irrepressible agent, Laurie Fox, is the sustainable fuel in my rocket, and it's thanks to her that I'm living on the Moon with a herd of space cats right now.

I owe much to early readers Charlie Jane Anders and Alan Henry, who made sure I wasn't saying anything wild or out of pocket. I'm eternally grateful to Erin Biba for stellar review and gentle guidance away from buffoonery. Cyrus Farivar, the intrepid journalist who knows everyone, introduced me to a key contact when I needed it. Thanks also to the librarians and archivists who helped me gain access to Paul Linebarger's papers and the SWORP archives.

I stayed the course with a lot of help from my beloved human companions Jesse Burns, Charlie Jane Anders, and Chris Palmer. You've been incredibly nice about listening to stories of trauma and terror for the past three years, and now it's time for a *Star Trek: Lower Decks* marathon.

Thanks, finally, to my readers. I hope you find peace in whatever way you can: in public works, in the arms of your loved ones, or in stories of a better world.

NOTES

PREFACE: THE BRAIN FOG OF WAR

1. Corley, Cheryl, "Floyd's Death Leads to Disinformation about Black Lives Matter Movement," NPR, May 25, 2021.
2. Vertuno, Jim, "Texas Man to Be Sentenced for Murder in Shooting at Black Lives Matter Protest," PBS, May 9, 2023.
3. Tameez, Hanaa', "OpenAI Will Give Local News Millions to Experiment with AI," Nieman Lab, July 18, 2023.
4. *A Guide to Researching the History of Psychological Operations*, Marquat Memorial Learning Resource Center, Fort Bragg, n.d.
5. "Carola," *Kirkus Reviews*, January 21, 1947.
6. Zats, Laura, and Erik Hane, "Critique, Awards, and Subjectivity," April 12, 2022, in *Print Run*, podcast.
7. Ray, Rashawn, "How 9/11 Helped to Militarize American Law Enforcement," Brookings Institute blog, September 9, 2021.
8. Pomerantsev, Peter, *This Is Not Propaganda: Adventures in the War against Reality* (PublicAffairs, 2019).
9. Sun Tzu, *The Art of War: A New Translation*, trans. Michael Nylan (W. W. Norton, 2020).

10. Kiesling, Eugenia, "On War without the Fog," *Military Review*, September–October 2001.

11. Hale, Lonsdale Augustus, "The Fog of War," Aldershot Military Society, 1896.

12. Lere, Philip, "Fog, Friction, and Logistics," US Army website, 2017. https://www.army.mil/article/185864/fog_friction_and_logistics.

13. Tracy, Jared M., "100 Years of Subterfuge: The History of Army Psychological Operations," US Army website, 2018. https://www.army.mil/article/199431/100_years_of_subterfuge_the_history_of_army_psychological_operations.

14. "Military Information Support Operations Process," John F. Kennedy Special Warfare Center and School, United States Army, December 2014.

15. "8th Psychological Operations Group (Airborne)," United States Army Special Operations Command, accessed May 2023. https://www.soc.mil/8thMISG/8thPOGhome.html.

16. Personal interview with Alex Stamos (April 8, 2022). See also Parks, Miles, "Fact Check: Russian Interference Went Far beyond 'Facebook Ads' Kushner Described," NPR, April 24, 2019.

17. Herman, Judith Lewis, *Trauma and Recovery* (Pandora, 2015).

18. Malik, Nesrine, *We Need New Stories: The Myths That Subvert Freedom* (W. W. Norton, 2019).

CHAPTER 1: THE MIND BOMB

1. Laplanche, L., and J.-B. Pontalis, *The Language of Psychoanalysis* (W. W. Norton, 1973). See especially the authors' definitions of "ego" and "unconscious."

2. Held, Lisa, "Psychoanalysis Shapes Consumer Culture: Or How Sigmund Freud, His Nephew and a Box of Cigars Forever Changed American Marketing," *Monitor on Psychology* 40, no. 11 (December 2009). https://www.apa.org/monitor/2009/12/consumer.

3. Trudel, Dominique, "Revisiting the Origins of Communication Research: Walter Lippmann's WWII Adventure in Propaganda and Psychological Warfare," *International Journal of Communication* 11 (2017).

4. Bernays, Edward, "The Engineering of Consent," *Annals of the Academy of Political and Social Science* 250, no. 1 (March 1947).

5. Tye, Larry, "Watch Out for the Top Banana," *Cabinet* 23 (Fall 2006).

6. *US Army Psychological Operations History Handbook*, US Army Special Operations Command History Office, 2018. https://arsof-history.org/pdf/handbook_psyop.pdf.

7. Anderson, Scott, *The Quiet Americans: Four CIA Spies at the Dawn of the Cold War* (Doubleday, 2020), 371.

8. Linebarger, Paul M. A., *Psychological Warfare* (Coachwhip Publications, 2010), 49.

9. Linebarger, *Psychological Warfare*, 143.

10. From an interview with literary critic Gary K. Wolfe, conducted by the author.

11. Linebarger, *Psychological Warfare*, 313.

12. Linebarger, 276.

13. Linebarger, 275.

14. Nevala-Lee, Alec, *Astounding: John W. Campbell, Isaac Asimov, Robert A. Heinlein, L. Ron Hubbard, and the Golden Age of Science Fiction* (Harper Collins, 2019).

15. Founded by tech industry leaders including Stewart Brand and Peter Schwartz, the Global Business Network ran from the late 1980s to the late 2010s, running workshops (a few of which I attended in the 2000s) where experts—academics, journalists, authors, and community leaders—briefed US intelligence agents on emerging threats and social practices online.

16. Linebarger, *Psychological Warfare*, 128–55.

17. Linebarger, 119.

18. "The Rise and Fall of Lord Haw Haw during the Second World War," Imperial War Museums. https://www.iwm.org.uk/history/the-rise-and-fall-of-lord-haw-haw-during-the-second-world-war.

19. Thwaites, Sam, "Germany Calling! Lord Haw Haw's Mic Is up for Sale," *Express*, August 26, 2009.

20. Taken from a recording of a 1940 broadcast. Joyce, William, *Lord Haw Haw (Germany Calling)*, YouTube video.

21. "Treason: American Lord Haw-Haw," *Time*, July 7, 1947.

22. Linebarger, *Psychological Warfare*, 161.

23. Linebarger, 153.

24. Linebarger, 154.

25. Saunders, Frances Stonor, *The Cultural Cold War* (The New Press, 2013).

26. Wolfe, Audra J., *Freedom's Laboratory: The Cold War Struggle for the Soul of Science* (Johns Hopkins University Press, 2018).

27. According to Sonya Lee, a reference specialist on Asia at the Library of Congress, over 2.4 billion leaflets were dropped on North and South Korea between 1950 and 1953. Lee, Sonya, "Korean War Propaganda Leaflet Collection at the Library of Congress," *4 Corners of the World* (blog), Library of Congress, September 26, 2017.

28. Jacobson, Mark, "'Minds Then Hearts': U.S. Political and Psychological Warfare during the Korean War," PhD diss., Ohio State University, 2005. OhioLINK Electronic Theses and Dissertations Center, http://rave.ohiolink.edu/etdc/view?acc_num=osu1108407385.

29. Boissoneault, Lorraine, "The True Story of Brainwashing and How It Shaped America," *Smithsonian Magazine*, May 22, 2017.

30. Holmes, Marcia, "Edward Hunter and the Origins of 'Brainwashing,'" Hidden Persuaders Project blog, May 26, 2017.

31. Hadley, David P., *The Rising Clamor: The American Press, the Central Intelligence Agency, and the Cold War* (University Press of Kentucky, 2019).

32. In Holmes, "Edward Hunter and the Origins," the author describes visiting the Edward Hunter papers at the Wisconsin Historical Society Archives, where she read Hunter's correspondence related to his dispute with *Time*.

33. Linebarger, Paul, "Possible Operations Research in FEC Psychological Warfare," ORO Technical Memorandum, ORO-T-2(FEC), September 14, 1950, excerpted in Appendix 20, *Opinion of George Cooper, Q.C., Regarding Canadian Government Funding of the Allan Memorial Institute in the 1950s and 1960s.*

34. Derksen, Maarten, "Manipulation Out of Control: J.A.M. Meerloo's 'Menticide,'" Hidden Persuaders Project blog, January 26, 2018. http://www7.bbk.ac.uk/hiddenpersuaders/blog/manipulation-out-of-control/.

35. Lemov, Rebecca, "Brainwashing's Avatar: The Curious Career of Dr. Ewen Cameron," *Grey Room* 45 (2011): 61–87.
36. This book is among his papers at the Hoover Institution Archives.
37. Lemov, "Brainwashing's Avatar."
38. McLuhan, Marshall, "Weapons: War of the Icons," in *Understanding Media* (McGraw-Hill, 1964).

CHAPTER 2: A FAKE FRONTIER

1. Harrington, Hugh T., "Propaganda Warfare: Benjamin Franklin Fakes a Newspaper," *Journal of the American Revolution*, November 10, 2014.
2. A text version of the *Supplement* is available from The Papers of Benjamin Franklin, sponsored by the American Philosophical Society and Yale University. https://franklinpapers.org/framedVolumes.jsp?vol =37&page=184a.
3. Parkinson, Robert G., "Fake News? That's a Very Old Story," *Washington Post*, November 25, 2016.
4. These numbers are estimates, based on incomplete data. Recent statistical analysis of battlefield deaths suggests that the casualties hovered around a million; other estimates are far higher, around ten million, because they account for death from disease and forced relocation. For the battlefield numbers, see Gillespie, Colin S., "Estimating the Number of Casualties in the American Indian War: A Bayesian Analysis Using the Power Law Distribution," *Annals of Applied Statistics* 11, no. 4 (December 2017): 2357–74. For the higher number including externalities, see Smith, David Michael, "Counting the Dead: Estimating the Loss of Life in the Indigenous Holocaust, 1492–Present," in *Representations and Realities: Proceedings of the Twelfth Native American Symposium*, ed. Mark B. Spencer (Southeastern Oklahoma State University, 2018).
5. See Blackhawk, Ned, *Violence over the Land: Indians and Empires in the Early American West* (Harvard University Press, 2008). I am also using the words "Indian" and "Indigenous" interchangeably here to refer to the diverse nations and tribes who lived on lands seized by the US government.

6. Deloria, Philip, "The Invention of Thanksgiving," *The New Yorker*, November 18, 2019.

7. "Myth of the 'Vanishing Indian,'" Pluralism Project, Harvard University, n.d.

8. See historical US census documents that list the cost of Indian Wars by year up through the 1840s: United States Department of the Interior, Census Office, "Indian Wars and Their Cost, and Civil Expenditures for Indians," in *Report on Indians Taxed and Indians Not Taxed in the United States at the Eleventh Census: 1890* (U.S. Government Printing Office, 1894). https://www2.census.gov/prod2/decennial/documents/1890a_v10-32.pdf.

9. Brennan, Natasha, "Justice for Ishi: UC Removes Hall's Name," *Indian Country Today*, March 16, 2021. https://indiancountrytoday.com/news/justice-for-ishi-uc-removes-halls-name.

10. See the Mohican Tribe website, Stockbridge-Munsee Community Band of Mohican Indians: https://www.mohican.com/.

11. Hughes, Michael A., "Military, Nineteenth Century," Encyclopedia of Oklahoma History and Culture, Oklahoma Historical Society. www.okhistory.org/publications/enc/entry.php?entry=MI025.

12. Schake, Kori, "Lessons from the Indian Wars," Hoover Institution, February 1, 2013.

13. The Indian Removal Act of 1830, found in "A Century of Lawmaking for a New Nation: U.S. Congressional Documents and Debates, 1774 to 1875," Library of Congress. https://www.loc.gov/collections/century-of-lawmaking/articles-and-essays/.

14. De Tocqueville, Alexis, *Democracy in America* (Knopf, 1994), chap. 18.

15. "Indian Emigration. We publish below the law of the United States for the appointment of Commission," September 8, 1832, *Cherokee Phoenix* vol. 5, no. 3, Hunter Library, Western Carolina University. www.wcu.edu/library/DigitalCollections/CherokeePhoenix/Vol5/no03/indian-emigration-we-publish-below-the-law-of-the-united-states-for-the-appointment-of-commission-page-2-column-1b.html.

16. Hicks, Brian, "The Cherokees vs. Andrew Jackson," *Smithsonian Magazine*, March 1, 2011.

17. Worcester v. Georgia, 31 U.S. 515 (1832). https://supreme.justia.com/cases/federal/us/31/515/.

18. Nelson, Sioban, "Historical Amnesia and Its Consequences: The Need to Build Histories of Practice," *Texto & Contexto—Enfermagem* 18, no. 4 (October 2009).

19. Rogin, Michael, "Make My Day! Spectacle as Amnesia in Imperial Politics," *Representations* 29 (1990): 99–123.

20. Coman, A., D. Manier, and W. Hirst, "Forgetting the Unforgettable through Conversation: Socially Shared Retrieval-Induced Forgetting of September 11 Memories," *Psychological Science* 20, no. 5 (2009): 627–33.

21. DeLay, Brian, "The U.S.–Mexican War: Forgotten Foes," *Berkeley Review of Latin American Studies*, Fall 2010.

22. Burnett, Peter, "State of the State Address." January 6, 1861, The Governors' Gallery, California State Library. https://governors.library.ca.gov/addresses/s_01-Burnett2.html.

23. Fuller, Thomas, "He Unleashed a California Massacre. Should This School Be Named for Him?," *New York Times*, October 27, 2021.

24. "Lake Mohonk Indian Conference," *New York Times*, October 14, 1892. www.nytimes.com/1892/10/14/archives/lake-mohonk-indian-conference.html.

25. Adams, David Wallace, *Education for Extinction: American Indians and the Boarding School Experience, 1875–1928* (University Press of Kansas, 2020).

26. Equal Justice Initiative, "March 3, 1819: Congress Allocates Funds to 'Civilize' Native American People," Calendar of Racial Injustice. https://calendar.eji.org/racial-injustice/mar/03.

27. In the SWORP archive, I found documents written by War Department officials about funding for kids to be sent by train from Oregon to other states.

28. Adams, *Education for Extinction*, 31.

29. Pember, Mary Annette, "Death by Civilization," *Atlantic*, March 8, 2019.

30. Associated Press, "U.S. Report Identifies Burial Sites Linked to Boarding Schools for Native Americans," NPR, May 11, 2022.

31. You can see photographs and hear recordings of the Ghost Dance on the Library of Congress website. Hall, Stephanie, "James Mooney Recordings of American Indian Ghost Dance Songs, 1894," *Folklife Today* (blog), Library of Congress, November 17, 2017.

32. Andersson, Rani-Henrik, *A Whirlwind Passed through Our Country: Lakota Voices of the Ghost Dance* (University of Oklahoma Press, 2019).

33. Estes, Nick, *Our History Is the Future: Standing Rock versus the Dakota Access Pipeline, and the Long Tradition of Indigenous Resistance* (Verso Books, 2023).

34. Fire, John, and Richard Erdoes, *Lame Deer: Seeker of Visions* (Simon & Schuster Paperbacks, 2009).

35. Estes, *Our History Is the Future*, 127.

36. Estes, 126.

37. "Ghost Dance Movement: Topics in Chronicling America," Library of Congress. https://guides.loc.gov/chronicling-america-ghost-dance-movement/selected-articles.

38. Sioux Indians, Wounded Knee Massacre: Hearings before the United States House Committee on Indian Affairs, Subcommittee on Indian Affairs, Seventy-Fifth Congress, third session, on March 7, May 12, 1938, pp. 2–3.

39. Mooney, James, "Death of Sitting Bull," in *The Ghost-Dance Religion and the Sioux Outbreak of 1890* (Government Printing Office, 1896), 856–57.

40. "Red Tomahawk Dies; Killed Sitting Bull; One-Time Member of Indian Police Succumbs at 82 on North Dakota Reservation," *New York Times*, August 9, 1931, 30.

41. Sioux Indians, Wounded Knee Massacre.

42. Estes, *Our History Is the Future*, 129.

43. Stillman, Deanne, "The Unlikely Alliance between Buffalo Bill and Sitting Bull," history.com, September 4, 2018.

44. Maddra, Sam Ann, *"Hostiles"? The Lakota Ghost Dance and the 1891–92 Tour of Britain by Buffalo Bill's Wild West* (University of Oklahoma Press, 2006).

45. Maddra, *Hostiles*, 206.

46. Maddra, 203.

47. Limerick, Patricia Nelson, *Something in the Soil: Legacies and Reckonings in the New West* (W. W. Norton, 2001).

48. Maddra, Sam, "The Wounded Knee Ghost Dance Shirt," *Journal of Museum Ethnography*, no. 8 (1996): 41–58.

49. "Glasgow's Ghost Dance Shirt," Andrew Hook Centre for American

Studies, University of Glasgow. www.gla.ac.uk/research/az/american studies/events/specialevents/drsammaddra/.

50. Isenberg, Andrew C., and Thomas Richards, "Alternative Wests: Rethinking Manifest Destiny," *Pacific Historical Review* 86, no. 1 (February 2017): 4–17.

51. Pratt, Julius W., "The Origin of 'Manifest Destiny,'" *American Historical Review* 32, no. 4 (July 1927): 795–98.

52. Smith, Henry Nash, *Virgin Land: The American West as Symbol and Myth* (Harvard University Press, 1970).

53. Turner, Frederick Jackson, "The Significance of the Frontier in American History," in *Proceedings of the State Historical Society of Wisconsin*, December 1893. https://www.historians.org/about-aha-and-member ship/aha-history-and-archives/historical-archives/the-significance -of-the-frontier-in-american-history-(1893).

54. Jackson, Helen Hunt, *A Century of Dishonor: Of the United States Government's Dealings with Some of the Indian Tribes* (Roberts Brothers, 1895).

55. Jackson, Helen Hunt, *Ramona* (n.p., 1884; Project Gutenberg, 2008). https://www.gutenberg.org/files/2802/2802-h/2802-h.htm.

CHAPTER 3: ADVERTISEMENTS FOR DISENFRANCHISEMENT

1. Newitz, Annalee, "How World War II Scientists Invented a Data-Driven Approach to Fighting Fascism," Ars Technica, June 3, 2016.

2. Confessore, Nicholas, and Danny Hakim, "Data Firm Says 'Secret Sauce' Aided Trump; Many Scoff," *New York Times*, March 6, 2017.

3. Cadwalladr, Carole, "'I Made Steve Bannon's Psychological Warfare Tool': Meet the Data War Whistleblower," *Guardian*, March 18, 2018.

4. Briant, Emma L., "As Cambridge Analytica and SCL Elections Shut Down, SCL Group's Defence Work Needs Real Scrutiny," Open Democracy, May 4, 2018.

5. Rosenberg, Matthew, Nicholas Confessore, and Carole Cadwalladr, "How Trump Consultants Exploited the Facebook Data of Millions," *New York Times*, March 17, 2018.

6. Mac, Ryan, "Cambridge Analytica Whistleblower Said He Wanted to Create 'NSA's Wet Dream,'" BuzzFeed News, March 22, 2018.

7. Rosenberg, Confessore, and Cadwalladr, "How Trump Consultants Exploited."

8. Wylie, Christopher, *Mindf*ck: Cambridge Analytica and the Plot to Break America* (Verbena Limited, 2019).

9. "Big Five Personality Test," Open-Source Psychometrics Project, August 2, 2019.

10. Rosenberg, Matthew, and Gabriel J. X. Dance, "'You Are the Product': Targeted by Cambridge Analytica on Facebook," *New York Times*, April 8, 2018.

11. Cadwalladr, "I Made Steve Bannon's Psychological Warfare Tool."

12. Jones, D. N., and D. L. Paulhus, "Introducing the Short Dark Triad (SD3): A Brief Measure of Dark Personality Traits," *Assessment* 21, no. 1 (2014): 28–41.

13. All quotes in this paragraph come from Wylie's book *Mindf*ck*.

14. Rosenberg, Confessore, and Cadwalladr, "How Trump Consultants Exploited."

15. Wylie, *Mindf*ck*.

16. Wylie.

17. Habermas, Jürgen, *Legitimation Crisis*, trans. Thomas McCarthy (Beacon Press, 1975).

18. He shared a 2014 edition of the textbook with me, because it is no longer classified.

19. Maan, Ajit, *Narrative Warfare* (self-pub., CreateSpace, 2018).

20. Snyder, Russell, *Hearts and Mines: With the Marines in al Anbar; A Memoir of Psychological Warfare in Iraq* (self-pub., iUniverse, 2011).

21. "Information Operations for the Information Age: IO in Irregular Warfare," September 24, 2021, in *Irregular Warfare Podcast*. https://irregular -warfare-podcast.castos.com/podcasts/8707/episodes/information -operations-for-the-information-age-io-in-irregular-warfare.

22. C-Span, *1996: Hillary Clinton on "Superpredators*," YouTube video.

23. Channel 4 News Investigations Team, "Revealed: Trump Campaign Strategy to Deter Millions of Black Americans from Voting in 2016," Channel 4 News, September 28, 2020.

24. Krogstad, Jens Manuel, and Mark Hugo Lopez, "Black Voter Turnout

Fell in 2016, Even as a Record Number of Americans Cast Ballots," Pew Research Center, August 27, 2020.

25. Gordon, Brett R., Florian Zettelmeyer, Neha Bhargava, and Dan Chapsky, "A Comparison of Approaches to Advertising Measurement: Evidence from Big Field Experiments at Facebook," *Marketing Science* 38, no. 2 (2019): 193–225.

26. "Hand Grenade Fragments Were Found in the Bodies of Victims in Prigozhin's Plane Crash, Putin Claims," AP News, October 5, 2023.

27. Bump, Philip, "How Russian Agents Allegedly Hacked the DNC and Clinton's Campaign," *Washington Post*, October 23, 2021.

28. Aisch, Gregor, Jon Huang, and Cecilia Kang, "Dissecting the #PizzaGate Conspiracy Theories," *New York Times*, December 10, 2016.

29. Miller, Michael E., "The Pizzagate Gunman Is Out of Prison. Conspiracy Theories Are Out of Control," *Washington Post*, February 16, 2021.

30. Perlroth, Nicole, Sheera Frenkel, and Scott Shane, "Facebook Exit Hints at Dissent on Handling of Russian Trolls," *New York Times*, March 19, 2018.

31. Weedon, Jen, William Nuland, and Alex Stamos, "Information Operations and Facebook," Facebook, April 27, 2017. web.archive .org/web/20170428102334/https://fbnewsroomus.files.wordpress .com/2017/04/facebook-and-information-operations-v1.pdf.

32. Timberg, Craig, "Russian Hackers Who Stole DNC Emails Failed at Social Media. WikiLeaks Helped," *Washington Post*, November 13, 2019.

33. Al-Rawi, Ahmed, and Anis Rahman, "Manufacturing Rage: The Russian Internet Research Agency's Political Astroturfing on Social Media," *First Monday* 25, no. 9 (August 2020).

34. Allbright, Claire, "A Russian Facebook Page Organized a Protest in Texas. A Different Russian Page Launched the Counterprotest," *Texas Tribune*, November 1, 2017.

35. Thompson, Alex, "Why the Right Wing Has a Massive Advantage on Facebook," *Politico*, September 26, 2020.

36. Lima, Cristiano, "Instagram Reinstates Robert Kennedy Jr. after Launch of Presidential Bid," *Washington Post*, June 4, 2023.

37. Douek, Evelyn, "The 5th Circuit's Jawboning Ruling," September 12,

2023, in *Moderated Content*, podcast, Stanford Law School. https://law .stanford.edu/podcasts/the-5th-circuits-jawboning-ruling/.

38. Duffy, Clare, "YouTube Will Now Allow 2020 Election Denialism Content, in Policy Reversal," CNN, June 2, 2023.

39. "Meta Rolls Back Measures to Tackle Covid Misinformation," Reuters, June 16, 2023.

40. O'Sullivan, Donie, and Sean Lyngaas, "Meta Cut Election Teams Months before Threads Launch, Raising Concerns for 2024," CNN, July 11, 2023.

41. Siegelman, Wendy, "Chart: Emerdata Limited—The New Cambridge Analytica/SCL Group?," Medium, July 31, 2022.

42. Pavlova, Uliana, "Russian Oligarch Yevgeny Prigozhin Appears to Admit to US Election Interference," CNN, November 8, 2022.

43. Kayyem, Juliette, "There Are No Lone Wolves," *Washington Post*, August 5, 2019.

44. Löwenthal, Leo, and Norbert Guterman, *Prophets of Deceit: A Study of the Techniques of the American Agitator* (Verso, 2021; originally published 1949).

45. Linebarger, *Psychological Warfare*, 114.

46. Katz, Matt, "We Were Warned," March 18, 2022, in *On the Media*, podcast, WNYC Studios. https://www.wnycstudios.org/podcasts/otm/episodes/on-the-media-we-were-warned.

CHAPTER 4: BAD BRAINS

1. Cornelius, Janet, "'We Slipped and Learned to Read': Slave Accounts of the Literacy Process, 1830–1865," *Phylon (1960–)* 44, no. 3 (1983): 171–86.

2. Iqbal, Saima S., "Louis Agassiz, under a Microscope," *Harvard Crimson*, March 18, 2021.

3. Fraser, Steven, ed., *The Bell Curve Wars: Race, Intelligence, and the Future of America* (Basic Books, 2008; originally published 1995).

4. Lemann, Nicholas, "The Bell Curve Flattened," *Slate*, January 18, 1997.

5. For more on how to access the NLS data, especially what is available to the public and what is restricted, see "Accessing NLS Data" on the Bureau of Labor Statistics' National Longitudinal Surveys website.

6. The book was published before gay marriage was legalized in the United States, so marriage meant strictly heterosexual unions.

7. Rushton, J. P., "Race, IQ, and the APA Report on *The Bell Curve*," *American Psychologist* 52, no. 1 (1997): 69–70.

8. See, for example, Jacoby, Russell, and Naomi Glauberman, eds., *The Bell Curve Debate: History, Documents, Opinions* (Times Books, 1998); and Fraser, *The Bell Curve Wars*.

9. Samuelson, Robert J., "'Bell Curve' Ballistics," *Washington Post*, October 26, 1994.

10. Broder, John M., "Clinton Rejects Racially Based Theory on IQs," *Los Angeles Times*, October 22, 1994.

11. Hemmer, Nicole, *Partisans: The Conservative Revolutionaries Who Remade American Politics in the 1990s* (Basic Books, 2022).

12. Sacks, David, and Peter Thiel, "The Case against Affirmative Action," *Stanford Magazine*, September/October 1996.

13. Watanabe, Teresa, "California Banned Affirmative Action in 1996. Inside the UC Struggle for Diversity," *Los Angeles Times*, October 31, 2022.

14. Siegel, Eric, "The Real Problem with Charles Murray and 'The Bell Curve,'" *Voices* (blog), Scientific American Blog Network, April 12, 2017.

15. See, for example, the *Bell Curve* debunker video from filmmaker Shaun, which has nearly three million views: https://www.youtube.com/watch?v=UBc7qBS1Ujo.

16. Herrnstein, Richard J., and Charles Murray, *The Bell Curve* (Free Press, 1994), 100.

17. This is quoted in DeParle, Jason, "Daring Research or 'Social Science Pornography'? Charles Murray," *New York Times Magazine*, October 9, 1994.

18. Interestingly, *Idiocracy* is a riff on a satirical short story called "The Marching Morons," published by Cyril M. Kornbluth in 1951, so this fantasy has deep roots in America.

19. Richardson, Ken, and Sarah H. Norgate, "Does IQ Really Predict Job Performance?," *Applied Developmental Science* 19, no. 3 (July 3, 2015): 153–69. See also Thomson, Jonny, "Is IQ a Load of BS?," Big Think, November 2, 2022.

20. Kamin, Leon J., *The Science and Politics of IQ* (Routledge, 1974).

21. Bond, Horace Mann, "Intelligence Tests and Propaganda," *Crisis* 28 (1924): 61–64.

22. Thomas, William B., "Black Intellectuals on IQ Tests," in Jacoby and Glauberman, *Bell Curve Debate.*

23. Jacoby and Glauberman, *Bell Curve Debate.*

24. Herrnstein and Murray, *Bell Curve*, 570.

25. See a complete discussion of *Mankind Quarterly*'s history and connection to eugenics in Angela Saini, *Superior: The Return of Race Science* (Beacon Press, 2019). See also Morgan Gstalter, "University of Arizona Accepted $458K from Eugenics Foundation: Report," *The Hill*, August 25, 2018.

26. Belew, Kathleen, "What Is White Replacement Theory? Explaining the White Supremacist Rhetoric," interview by Lulu Garcia-Navarro, NPR, September 26, 2021.

27. All quotes from Saini here come from the author's podcast interview with her "The Legacy of Scientific Racism," in *Our Opinions Are Correct*, December 19, 2019. https://www.ouropinionsarecorrect.com/shownotes/2019/12/19/episode-47-the-legacy-of-scientific-racism.

28. DeParle, "Daring Research."

29. Herrnstein and Murray, *Bell Curve*, 263.

30. Herrnstein and Murray, 339.

31. Herrnstein and Murray, 327.

32. From DeParle, "Daring Research."

33. Herrnstein and Murray, *Bell Curve*, 509.

34. Herrnstein and Murray, 526.

35. Stern, Michael, "A Dystopian Fable," in Jacoby and Glauberman, *Bell Curve Debate.*

36. Herrnstein and Murray, *Bell Curve*, 551.

37. Frank, Jeffrey A., "Black and White & Read All Over: The Hot Books That Make the Melting Pot Boil," *Washington Post*, September 22, 1995.

38. Hunter, Edward, *Brainwashing: The Story of Men Who Defied It* (Forgotten Books, 2012), 108.

39. Hunter, *Brainwashing*, 112.

40. For a good example of ideas from the human-biodiversity movement,

see Wade, Nicholas J., *A Troublesome Inheritance: Genes, Race, and the Rise of the West* (Penguin, 2014).

41. Coop, Graham, Michael B. Eisen, Rasmus Nielsen, Molly Przeworski, and Noah Rosenberg, letter to the editor, *New York Times*, August 8, 2014.

42. Yglesias, Matthew, "The Bell Curve Is about Policy. And It's Wrong," Vox, April 10, 2018.

43. El-Mohtar, Amal, "Calling for the Expulsion of Theodore Beale from SFWA," personal website, June 13, 2013. https://amalelmohtar.com/calling-for-the-expulsion-of-theodore-beale-from-sfwa/.

44. Hines, Jim C., "Racist Takes Dump in SFWA Twitter Stream: News at 11," personal website, June 13, 2013. https://www.jimchines.com/2013/06/racist-takes-dump-in-sfwa-twitter-stream-news-at-11/.

45. Cunningham, Joel, "Read N. K. Jemisin's Historic Hugo Speech," *B&N Reads*, Barnes and Noble, November 6, 2021. www.barnesandnoble.com/blog/sci-fi-fantasy/read-n-k-jemisins-historic-hugo-speech.

CHAPTER 5: SCHOOL RULES

1. Kirchick, James, *Secret City: The Hidden History of Gay Washington* (Henry Holt, 2022).

2. Yagoda, Ben, "What Drove Sigmund Freud to Write a Scandalous Biography of Woodrow Wilson?," *Smithsonian Magazine*, September 1, 2018.

3. Adkins, Judith, "'These People Are Frightened to Death': Congressional Investigations and the Lavender Scare," *Prologue Magazine* 48, no. 2 (Summer 2016).

4. See US Census data here: https://data.census.gov/table?g=1600000US4837000&tid=DECENNIALPL2020.P2.

5. Hernández, Magda (@IISDMagdaHdz), Twitter, July 25, 2021, 5:11 p.m. https://twitter.com/IISDMagdaHdz/status/1419435247310147584.

6. Caldon, Elle LeeAnne, "We Will Not Back Down," *Dallas Voice*, December 9, 2021.

7. Lopez, Brian, "North Texas Principal Resigns to End Fight over Whether He Was Teaching 'Critical Race Theory,'" *Texas Tribune*, November 10, 2021.

8. Lopez, "North Texas Principal Resigns."

9. Irving ISD, "Below is Irving ISD's official statement regarding the protest at MacArthur High School today," Twitter, September 22, 2021, 5:06 p.m. https://twitter.com/irvingisd/status/144081466748443443 6?s=21.

10. You can see a video recording of the full hearing on the school board website, Irving Schools Television. http://istv.irvingisd.net/board-of -trustees/03222022-758.

11. Lanning, K., "The Evolution of Grooming: Concept and Term," *Journal of Interpersonal Violence* 33, no. 1 (2018): 5–16.

12. Charles, Douglas M., *Hoover's War on Gays: Exposing the FBI's "Sex Deviates" Program* (University Press of Kansas, 2015).

13. Eugenios, Jillian, "How 1970s Christian Crusader Anita Bryant Helped Spawn Florida's LGBTQ Culture War," NBCNews.com, April 14, 2022.

14. Bryant, Anita, *The Anita Bryant Story: The Survival of Our Nation's Families and the Threat of Militant Homosexuality* (Spire Books, 1977).

15. Block, Melissa, "Accusations of 'Grooming' Are the Latest Political Attack—with Homophobic Origins," NPR, May 11, 2022.

16. The bill originally focused on elementary school children, but was subsequently expanded. See: Yurcaba, Jo, "DeSantis Signs 'Don't Say Gay' Expansion and Gender-Affirming Care Ban," NBCNews.com, May 17, 2023.

17. Jones, Dustin, and Jonathan Franklin, "Not Just Florida. More Than a Dozen States Propose So-Called 'Don't Say Gay' Bills," NPR, April 10, 2022.

18. Pushaw, Christina, "If you're against the Anti-Grooming Bill, you are probably a groomer or at least you don't denounce the grooming of 4–8 year old children. Silence is complicity," Twitter, March 4, 2022, 4:33 p.m. https://twitter.com/ChristinaPushaw/status/14998907196910510 08?s=20&t=hJN8uChmyETqe2Vdbim-QQ.

19. Yoon, John, "Transgender Influencer Speaks Out after Backlash against Bud Light," *New York Times*, June 29, 2023.

20. Vogels, Emily A., "The State of Online Harassment," Pew Research Center: Internet, Science & Tech, January 13, 2021.

21. Ifill, Sherrilyn, "How This Supreme Court Is Changing the Rules of Law," interview by Dahlia Lithwick, *Amicus*, podcast, *Slate*, December 17,

2022. https://slate.com/podcasts/amicus/2022/12/civil-rights-lawyer -sherrilyn-ifill-on-how-arguments-are-going-down-at-this-supreme -court.

22. This was Southwestern Law School professor Hila Keren, an expert on business and contract law. See Keren, Hila, "The Blockbuster Case You Probably Haven't Heard about on Apple Podcasts," interview by Dahlia Lithwick, *Amicus*, podcast, *Slate*, December 3, 2022. https://podcasts .apple.com/us/podcast/the-blockbuster-case-you-probably-havent -heard-about/id928790786?i=1000588574748.

23. Bahari, Sarah, "Irving Teacher Who Supported Gay Pride Symbols in School Says Her Contract Will Be Terminated," *Dallas News*, April 8, 2022.

24. Zeeble, Bill, "Protestors Say Embattled Irving High School Teacher Who Put Up Rainbow Stickers Should Keep Her Job," KERA News, April 19, 2022.

25. Friedman, Jonathan, and Nadine Farid Johnson, "Banned in the USA: The Growing Movement to Ban Books," PEN America.

26. "2015 Book Challenges Infographic Long," American Library Association, July 18, 2017.

27. "The California Report," KQED, November 17, 2022.

28. "Facts about LGBTQ Youth Suicide," The Trevor Project, December 15, 2021.

CHAPTER 6: DIRTY COMICS

1. Jay, Alex, "Comics: Marjorie Wilkes Huntley," *Tenth Letter of the Alphabet*, November 17, 2014.

2. Lepore, Jill, *The Secret Life of Wonder Woman* (Vintage, 2014).

3. Associated Press, "Neglected Amazons to Rule Men in 1,000 Yrs, Says Psychologist," *Washington Post*, November 11, 1937.

4. Mandell, Wallace, "The Realization of an Idea," Johns Hopkins Bloomberg School of Public Health, 1995.

5. Smith, Ken, *Mental Hygiene: Classroom Films 1945–1970* (Blast Books, 1999).

6. "The Comics Code of 1954," Comic Book Legal Defense Fund.

7. González, Jennifer, "The Senate Comic Book Hearings of 1954," *In Custodia Legis* (blog), Library of Congress, October 26, 2022.

8. Wright-Mendoza, Jessie, "Richard Wright Helped Bring Mental Healthcare to Harlem," JSTOR Daily, April 6, 2019.

9. Wood, Erika, "NY's Jim Crow Laws: Back in the Day, and What Remains Today," Brennan Center for Justice, March 1, 2010.

10. Tilley, Carol L., "Seducing the Innocent: Fredric Wertham and the Falsifications That Helped Condemn Comics," *Information & Culture* 47, no. 4 (2012): 383–413.

11. Wertham, Fredric, *Seduction of the Innocent* (Rinehart & Company, 1954), 97.

12. Wertham, *Seduction of the Innocent*, 34.

13. Wertham, 167.

14. Wertham, 234.

15. Wertham, 233.

16. Tilley, "Seducing the Innocent."

17. Simone, Gail, "The History," in "Fan Gail Simone Responds," Women in Refrigerators.

18. Waid, Mark, "Mark Waid Responds," Women in Refrigerators.

19. Millar, Mark, "Mark Millar Responds," Women in Refrigerators.

20. Anders, Charlie, "Supergirls Gone Wild: Gender Bias in Comics Shortchanges Superwomen," *Mother Jones*, July 30, 2007.

21. Sharf, Zack, "Kelly Marie Tran: Star Wars Fan Harassment Felt Like an 'Embarrassingly Horrible Breakup,'" IndieWire, March 4, 2021.

22. Sun, Rebecca, "The Resurrection of Kelly Marie Tran: On Surviving 'Star Wars' Bullying, the Pressures of Representation, and 'Raya and the Last Dragon,'" *Hollywood Reporter*, August 5, 2021.

23. Roth, Emma, "Amazon's Putting a Three-Day Pause on Reviews for the Rings of Power," Verge, September 4, 2022.

24. Romano, Aja, "The Racist Backlash to The Little Mermaid and Lord of the Rings Is Exhausting and Extremely Predictable," Vox, September 17, 2022.

25. DePass, Tanya, "In Fantasy Worlds, Historical Accuracy Is a Lie," Boing Boing, October 30, 2015.

26. Lee, Wendy, "'The Lord of the Rings' Cast Denounces Threats to

Nonwhite Actors Depicting Middle-Earth Characters," *Los Angeles Times*, September 8, 2022.

27. Linebarger, *Psychological Warfare*, 172.

28. "Word of the Year 2022," Merriam-Webster, accessed September 20, 2023.

CHAPTER 7: HISTORY IS A GIFT

1. Inter-Agency Working Group on DDR, *Operational Guide to the Integrated Disarmament, Demobilization and Reintegration Standards* (United Nations, 2010).

2. Linebarger, *Psychological Warfare*, 314–15.

3. Linebarger, 318.

4. Younker, Jason, "The Southwest Oregon Research Project: Strengthening Coquille Sovereignty with Archival Research and Gift Giving," *American Indian Culture and Research Journal* 29, no. 2 (2005): 1.

5. See the map in the National Archives digital catalog: https://catalog.archives.gov/id/50926100.

6. "Indigenous Data Sovereignty," "Research Guides: Indigenous Studies," University of Toronto Libraries, accessed September 1, 2023. https://guides.library.utoronto.ca/indigenousstudies/datasovereignty.

7. O'Neal, J. R., "The Right to Know: Decolonizing Native American Archives," *Journal of Western Archives* 6, no. 1 (2015).

8. Gupta, Meghanlata, "Regaining Control: Indigenous-Owned and Operated Archives," *Indian Country Today*, January 29, 2022.

9. "Indigenous Digital Archive," Museum of Indian Arts & Culture, accessed September 1, 2023.

10. Lewis, David G., "Natives in the Nation's Archives: The Southwest Oregon Research Project," *Journal of Western Archives* 6, no. 1 (2015).

CHAPTER 8: DEPROGRAMMING FOR DEMOCRACY

1. Engler, Alex, "How Platforms Can Prevent Misinformation Like #dcblackout," Lawfare, June 15, 2020. www.lawfaremedia.org/article/how-platforms-can-prevent-misinformation-dcblackout.

2. Timberg, Craig, Elizabeth Dwoskin, and Fenit Nirappil, "Twitter

Became a Major Vehicle for Misinformation about Unrest in D.C.," *Washington Post*, June 1, 2020.

3. Katy (@kathrynroseee), "Search the latest tweets with 'who has friends telecommuting into DC' I want to know what really happened? #dcblackout #dcsafe," Twitter, June 1, 2020, 8:03 a.m. https://twitter.com/kathrynroseee/status/1267456866856157185.

4. Alizadeh, Meysam, Jacob N. Shapiro, Cody Buntain, and Joshua A. Tucker, "Content-Based Features Predict Social Media Influence Operations," *Science Advances* 6, no. 30 (July 22, 2020).

5. See, for example: Newcomb, Alyssa, "A Timeline of Facebook's Privacy Issues—and Its Responses," NBCNews.com, March 24, 2018; and Heiligenstein, Michael X., "Facebook Data Breaches: Full Timeline through 2023," *Firewall Times*, May 31, 2023.

6. Mac, Ryan, and Charlie Warzel, "Departing Facebook Security Officer's Memo: 'We Need to Be Willing to Pick Sides,'" BuzzFeed News, July 24, 2018.

7. Center for an Informed Public, Digital Forensic Research Lab, Graphika, and Stanford Internet Observatory, "The Long Fuse: Misinformation and the 2020 Election," Stanford Digital Repository: Election Integrity Partnership, v1.3.0 (2021). Available at https://purl.stanford.edu/tr171zs0069.

8. Nguyen, Tina, and Mark Scott, "How 'Sharpiegate' Went from Online Chatter to Trumpworld Strategy in Arizona," *Politico*, November 5, 2020.

9. Martin, Nick, "A QAnon candidate for Arizona governor in 2022 is organizing a #SharpieGate protest on Friday at the state capitol. 'Bring your Sharpies and hold them high,'" Twitter, November 4, 2020, 1:54 p.m. https://twitter.com/nickmartin/status/1324092697288691712.

10. Election Integrity Partnership Team, "Repeat Offenders: Voting Misinformation on Twitter in the 2020 United States Election," Election Integrity Partnership, June 24, 2022.

11. Schneier, Bruce, "Toward an Information Operations Kill Chain," Lawfare, April 24, 2019.

12. Newitz, Annalee, "A Better Internet Is Waiting for Us," *New York Times*, November 30, 2019.

13. Lorenz, Taylor, "Twitter vs. Threads, and Why Influencers Could Be the Ultimate Winners," interview by Brittany Luse, *It's Been a Minute*, podcast, NPR, July 19, 2023.
14. Meyer, Michelle N., "Everything You Need to Know about Facebook's Controversial Emotion Experiment," *Wired*, June 30, 2014.
15. Schneier, "Toward an Information Operations Kill Chain."
16. Shendruk, Amanda, and Alexandra Ossola, "Welcome to Leeside, the US's First Climate Haven," Quartz, September 1, 2020.

CHAPTER 9: PUBLIC SPHERES OF THE FUTURE

1. Klinenberg, Eric, *Palaces for the People: How Social Infrastructure Can Help Fight Inequality, Polarization, and the Decline of Civic Life* (Crown, 2018).
2. Prelinger, Megan, *Another Science Fiction: Advertising the Space Race, 1957–1962* (Blast Books, 2010).

INDEX